W9-BVU-773

WHAT THE JUDGE THOUGHT

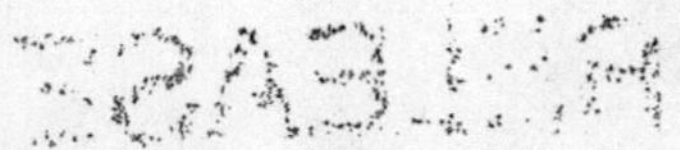

WHAT THE JUDGE THOUGHT

By

HIS HONOUR JUDGE

EDWARD ABBOTT PARRY

Let us consider the reasons of the case, for nothing is law that is not reason.

Sir John Powell,
Coggs v. *Bernard.* 2 *Lord Raymond*, 911.

Essay Index Reprint Series

BOOKS FOR LIBRARIES PRESS
FREEPORT, NEW YORK

First Published 1923
Reprinted 1968

LIBRARY OF CONGRESS CATALOG CARD NUMBER:
68-29237

PRINTED IN THE UNITED STATES OF AMERICA

TO

MY FRIEND AND COLLEAGUE

WILLIAM BURCHELL PRITCHARD

Contents

What the Judge Thought

Chapter I: *Concerning Abraham Lincoln*

OF the log-cabin life of Abraham Lincoln, from his birth in 1809 to his election for Legislature in 1834, every schoolboy knows something. The stories of the heroism of his early life are parables in cottage homes on both sides of the Atlantic. In the same way every one is familiar with the great drama of his career as President, with its terrible scenes of war and final tragedy of murder. Told and retold in memoirs, histories, poetry, and fiction, there is already a halo of literature around Lincoln that only shines on the great figures of the world.

It is somewhat surprising that—in this country, at all events—so little is known about his career as an advocate, which from 1836 to 1860 occupied the best years of his life. Joseph Choate, speaking at Edinburgh, told us: "I lay great stress on Lincoln's career as a lawyer—much more than his biographers do; I am sure his training and experience in the Courts had much to do with the developments of those forces of intellect and character which he soon displayed in a wider area." Our good ambassador was right, but he did not trouble us with the reason of this neglect, though no doubt his critical insight had diagnosed it. The fact is that it is distasteful to the average man to find that his hero is a lawyer, and Lincoln's biographers and historians, who with true literary instinct please to write and write to please, have allowed his twenty-four years of professional life to become a colourless background to the stirring story of his political career that they may please the groundlings who have a high-souled hatred of the lawyer politician. Although we may not go all the way with an American writer who says, "if Abraham Lincoln had not commenced lawyer he would not have concluded President," yet the story of his professional life must contribute to our power of appreciating the character of the man and to a better understanding of the circumstances in which his genius was able to take root and flourish.

To a writer on the disadvantages of education, Abraham Lincoln is a human text. His schooling was of the scantiest. At some time or another every man must become his own schoolmaster if he seeks education Abraham Lincoln began at once, and continued directing his own studies all the days of his life. At the age of fourteen fortune had endowed him with the Bible, "Æsop's Fables," "Robinson Crusoe," and "Pilgrim's Progress." There was also a "History of the United States" and "Life of Washington." He not only read his library, but he learnt it by heart. You can trace in his writings the directness and simplicity of Defoe and Bunyan, his love of apt parable may have been derived from Æsop, and the Bible confirmed his natural instinct for right action and strengthened his passionate love of honesty.

From the earliest he was an ardent student. He collected every scrap of paper he could find to make a commonplace book of extracts from volumes lent to him to read. He studied in the fields, under the trees, and by the waning firelight when all were asleep. His notebook was the boarded wall of the cabin, his stylograph a lump of chalk. An old farmer recalls him sitting barefoot on a wood pile reading a book. This being such an extraordinary proceeding for a farm hand, he asked him what he was reading.

" I'm not reading," replied Lincoln, " I'm studying."

" Studying what ? " asked the farmer.

" Law, sir," was the dignified reply.

" Great God Almighty ! " ejaculated the farmer in an outburst of stupefied piety, and went his way in amazement.

But years afterwards he was the honoured possessor of a true story of a great hero, and biographers made pilgrimages to hear the old man tell it.

In 1833 a disastrous partnership in a small store came to an untimely end, leaving Lincoln with a legacy of debt which he honourably paid off in succeeding years. He was now four-and-twenty, and the only asset of the business he retained was a copy of " Blackstone's Commentaries," which he had found at the bottom of a barrel of household débris which the firm had purchased at a sale. He borrowed other law books, and is said at this time to have possessed an old volume of Indiana statutes which he learned by heart and used to quote effectively in later years. He acted as a sort of " next friend " to parties before the local justices of the peace, and drew mortgages and contracts for his neighbours, though he does not seem to have received pay for these services. It was the only apprenticeship to the Law that he could afford, and he became an articled clerk to himself, so to speak.

By turns he was a store clerk, surveyor, and postmaster at New Salem until 1834, when he was elected to the Legislature, and had to borrow two hundred dollars to buy clothing to be fit for his new dignity. On March 24th, 1836, he became legally qualified to practise the law, and left New Salem to settle in the county town of Springfield, and entered into partnership with a lawyer from Kentucky, J. T. Stuart, who had already shown him much kindness.

The story of his coming to Springfield is told by his friend Joshua Speed, a prosperous young merchant of the town, to whom he went on his first arrival. " He had ridden into the town," writes Speed, " on a borrowed horse and engaged from the only cabinet-maker in the village a single bedstead. He came on to my store, set his saddle-bags on the counter, and inquired what the furniture of a single bedstead would cost. I took slate and pencil, made a calculation, and found the sum for furniture complete would amount to seventeen dollars in all.

" Said he, ' It is probably cheap enough ; but I want to say that cheap as it is I have not the money to pay, but if you will credit me until Christmas and my experiment here as a lawyer is a success, I will pay you then. If I fail in that, I will probably never pay you at all.' "

The good Speed was so touched by the melancholy tones in which he spoke of possible failure that he offered him a share of his own room, which contained a large double bed.

"Where is your room?" asked Lincoln.

"Upstairs," said his friend, pointing to a stairway that led out of the store.

Lincoln hitched up his saddle-bags, ran upstairs, and took possession of his room, returning in a few moments, smiling contentedly, and announced: "Well, Speed, I'm moved."

One of Speed's store clerks was William H. Herndon, for whom Lincoln had a great affection. He also slept in the big room over the store, and the three young friends were all earnest in politics, study, and debate. On leaving Stuart, Lincoln became partner with Stephen T. Logan for a few years, until both were running for Congress, when they parted in a friendly spirit, and Lincoln was on his own. It was then, in 1845, that he proposed to his young friend Herndon that he should come into partnership with him. The young man hung back on the ground of want of practice and inexperience, but Lincoln clinched the matter in his kindly, masterful way, saying: "Billy, I can trust you, if you will trust me." Billy and Abraham were Jonathan and David through sixteen years of practice in the law, and it is through his junior partner's reminiscences that we gain the most intimate picture of Lincoln the advocate.

To appreciate fully the power of Lincoln among the

lawyers of his day, we must not forget how different were the circumstances of the administration of justice from anything our generation has experienced. Lincoln had seen even rougher courts of justice than those he practised in. We know that as a lad he used to haunt the Boonville Court-house whenever a trial was forward, and years afterwards, at the White House, reminded Breckenridge the advocate that he had heard him defend a murderer there. " I concluded," said Lincoln, " that if I could ever make as good a speech as that, my soul would be satisfied, for it was the best I had ever heard." In these earliest days the Court-house was merely a log hut, and the hunters and trappers who formed the jury retired into the woods to consider their verdict.

Mr. Hill, in his admirable essay on " Lincoln the Lawyer "—a book too little known in this country—reports the address of a learned judge to the prisoner in " The People v. Green " to illustrate the manners of pioneer justice. " Mr. Green," began the learned judge very politely, " *the jury* in their verdict say you are guilty of murder, and the law says you are to be hung. Now, I want you and all your friends down on Indian Creek to know that it is not *I* who condemn you, but the *jury* and the *law*. Mr. Green, the law allows you time for preparation, so the Court wants to know what time you would like to be hung."

The prisoner " allowed " it made no difference to him, but His Honour did not appreciate this freedom of action.

" Mr. Green, you must know it is a very serious matter to be hung," he protested uneasily. " You'd better take all the time you can get. The Court will give you until this day four weeks."

The prosecutor thought this but a tame ending, and reminded the judge that the correct thing was to pronounce a formal sentence and exhort the prisoner to repentance.

"Not at all," interrupted the judge. "Mr. Green understands the whole matter as if I had preached to him for a month. He knows he's got to be hung this day four weeks. You understand it that way, don't you?"

Mr. Green nodded, and the Court adjourned.

Rough and ready as the formalities of justice might be, it was very necessary in the judge's own interest to make it clear that what he was administering was really law. Too much learning was apt to puzzle a backwoodsman jury, and Mr. Hill has another contemporary story of a foreman who returned to a learned judge to say his jury could not agree their verdict, and on being asked what the trouble was, replied: "Judge, this 'ere is the difficulty. The jury want to know if that thar what you told us was r'al'y the law or on'y jist your notion."

Even when Lincoln joined the Illinois Bar the courts were very primitive. The judge sat on a raised platform with a pine or whitewood board on which to write his notes. There was a small table on one side for the clerk, and a larger one, sometimes covered with green baize, for the lawyers who sat around and rested their feet on it. There were few law books. The Revised Statutes, the Illinois Form Book, and a few text-books might be found in most towns, but there were no extensive law libraries anywhere. From one Court-house to another the judge drove in a gig or buggy, the Bar following for the most part on horseback with a clean shirt and one or two elementary law books in their saddle-bags. Some too poor to ride tramped the circuit on foot, but as there were many horse thieves to defend, and a horse was a well-recognised fee, it was not long before a young man of ability was mounted.

Such was the circuit when Lincoln first joined it. He was then twenty-seven years of age, " six feet four inches in height, awkward, ungainly and apparently shy. He was dressed in ill-fitting homespun clothes, the trousers a little too short and the coat a trifle too large. He had the appearance of a rustic on his first visit to the circus." He kept his bank-book and the bulk of his letters in his hat, a silk plug, and a memo. would be jotted down on paper and stuck in the lining of his hat. No wonder Stanton, the courtly advocate of Chicago, sneered contemptuously at the " long-armed creature from Illinois," though he learned in the end to admire and respect him.

But the public recognised his capacity at once. In spite of physical and social drawbacks, Lincoln as an advocate was an immediate success. He was soon on one side or the other in every important case, and was pointed out to strangers by proud citizens of Springfield as " Abe Lincoln, the first lawyer of Illinois ! " He was a great favourite not only with the public, but with his fellow-lawyers on circuit. Although he never drank intoxicating liquor, and did not smoke or chew tobacco, he was fond of a horse-race or a cock-fight, and when addressing his fellow-countrymen drew his illustrations from these pursuits. There is an oft-told circuit memory of how he crushed a swaggering opponent who evaded his argument by saying that he reminded him of "Bap McNabb's rooster, who was splendidly groomed and trained for the fight, but when he was thrown in the ring, turned tail and fled, and Bap yelled after him, 'Yes, you little cuss, you're great on dress parade, but not worth a damn in a fight!'"

A further reason for his popularity was his gift as a teller of stories and jests full of the wit and character of the free, outspoken, primitive people from whom he sprang. Foolish people have tried to record some of these things, still more foolish folk have endeavoured to prove that their hero was too pure and unspotted from the world to trifle with such nonsense. Wiser minds wil recognise that since the world began the teller of a merry tale has never wanted for a jolly audience, and at the root of Lincoln's success with all sorts and conditions of men lay his gift of story-telling.

But the great qualities that brought him success as an advocate were his industry, honesty, and independence. Writing to a law student who had asked him the best method of studying law, he says: "The mode is very simple, though laborious and tedious. It is only to get books and read and study them carefully. Work, work, work, is the main thing." He himself used to read aloud when studying, for then, he said, "Two senses catch the idea; first I see what I read; second, I hear it, and therefore I can remember it better." "Billy" Herndon, his law partner—who plays the part of Boswell to his Johnson—draws a quaint picture of him at a circuit inn.

" We usually at the little country inns occupied the same bed. In most cases the beds were too short for him, and his feet would hang over the foot-board, thus exposing a limited expanse of shin bone. Placing a candle on a chair at the head of the bed, he would read and study for hours." His studies were by no means confined to law, and he never allowed his mind to become " case-ridden " ; indeed, one of his greatest qualities was his power to stand on his own and reason out for himself the true aspects of a case apart from what lawyers love to call " authorities."

But the foundation of his fame and success as an advocate was his honesty. As a friendly critic said, he was " perversely honest." The faithful " Billy " tells a story of his first appearance in the Supreme Court of Illinois, and quotes his words as follows : " This is the first case I have ever had in this Court, and I have therefore examined it with great care. As the Court will perceive by looking at the abstract of the record, the only question in the case is one of authority. I have not been able to find any authority to sustain my side of the case, but I have found several cases directly in point on the other side. I will now give these authorities to the Court and submit the case." Some biographers reject this story as improbable, and lawyers have criticised his conduct adversely. The question whether, if an advocate knows of a decided case in point against him, he ought or ought not to reveal it, has often been discussed. Joshua Williams, the Gamaliel of Real Property Law, boldly states : " It seems to me that in principle this is no part of his duty as an advocate " ; but he admits that if the judge asks him whether he knows of any case against him, he is bound to tell the truth. With all respect for so great an authority, I, for my part, am not convinced. If an advocate knows that the law is *x*, he has no right by acts of commission or omission to infer to the Court that it is *y*. I think we may accept " Billy's " story as true, and conclude that Lincoln not only took that course, but that it was the right course to take.

As long as a lawyer is ready to forgo fees, there is no reason why he should not ride his hobby-horse of honesty to his heart's content. Lincoln and Herndon as a firm set themselves out to conduct business on unusual lines, and maybe carried their ideals very far, but they made good. It was against their principles to contest a clear matter of right. If they thought a client was in the wrong, they told him so and sent him away. Even when they came to the conclusion that a client had a good case in law, they would not take it up if the moral aspect of it was cloudy. The following letter to a proposed client states Lincoln's views on the matter in his own words : " Yes, we can doubtless gain your case for you ; we can set a whole neighbourhood at loggerheads, we can distress a widowed mother and her six fatherless children, and thereby get for you six hundred dollars to which you seem to have a legal claim, but which rightfully belongs, it appears to me, as much to the woman and her children as it does to you. You must remember, however, that some things legally right are not morally right. We shall not take your case, but we will give you a little advice for which we will charge you nothing. You seem to be a sprightly, energetic man. We would advise you to try your hand at making six hundred dollars some other way."

Lincoln put his personal point of view very forcibly before a young law student who had qualms of conscience about joining the profession. "Let no young man choosing the law for a calling yield to that popular belief that honesty is not compatible with its practice. If in your judgment you cannot be an honest lawyer, resolve to be honest without being a lawyer."

Of necessity, therefore, Lincoln was not a successful advocate in any case unless he was convinced of its righteousness. His limitations were well known, and he was not often called upon to defend prisoners. He did everything in his power to examine carefully into his own clients' grounds of action, but clients are often self-deceivers and are apt not to tell the whole truth to their advisers. When Lincoln found in the middle of a trial that his client had lied to him, and that justice was opposed to him, he could no longer conduct the case with enthusiasm and courage. On one occasion he was appearing for a plaintiff, and in the middle of the case evidence was brought forward showing that his client was attempting a fraud. Lincoln rose up and went to his hotel. Presently the Judge sent for him, but he refused to come back, saying, "Tell the Judge my hands are dirty; I came over here to wash them." To him the maxim, "Come into court with clean hands," was a command to be obeyed in spirit and letter.

This way of doing business was the only possible one for him. He had a fundamental instinct for right action. He used to explain his necessity for taking whatever course he felt to be the right one in the following homely anecdote. He was riding on circuit and passed by a deep slough where he saw a wretched pig wallowing and struggling in the mud. It was clear to his mind that the animal could not release himself. However, the mud was deep, and Lincoln was wearing, what for him was unusual, a new suit of clothes. He rode on and left the pig to his fate. He could not get rid of the thought of the poor brute, and carried the picture of his death-struggle in his mind's eye. After riding on about two miles he turned back, waded into the mud, saved the pig, and spoiled his clothes. When he analysed his action, he said that this was really " selfishness, for he certainly went to the pig's relief in order to take a pain out of his own mind."

In the same way, to be connected even professionally with dishonesty was painful to him. It is curious, therefore, that many biographers have accepted a story told about the famous Armstrong case, when he defended the son of Hannah Armstrong, who had shown him much kindness in his early days at New Salem, in which Lincoln is made the hero of as cute and wicked a deception as was ever practised on a Court and jury. The charge was murder committed at night, and the case turned on identity. One of the witnesses who saw young Armstrong strike the fatal blow was asked by Lincoln how he managed to see so clearly, and replied, " By the moonlight," adding that " the moon was about in the same place that the sun would be at ten o'clock in the morning, and was almost full." On this Lincoln called to an usher for an almanac, and on its production it appeared that the moon set at midnight and was only slightly past its first quarter.

The charge against Lincoln was that he had given the usher the almanac to have by him and that it was an almanac of the previous year. That Lincoln should have risked such a cheat, and that counsel on the other side and the judge and jury should not have discovered it, is grossly improbable, but the recollection of those present and a reference to an actual almanac show that this story, which for many years had considerable currency, is a myth. Armstrong's life was saved by Lincoln's eloquence; he was pleading for the life of a child he had rocked in the cradle, the son of a woman who had mothered him in his youth, and he threw his heart and soul into the lad's defence.

To reproduce forensic eloquence by any form of literal illustration is scarcely possible. One wants the figure, the tone, the gesture, the crowded Court-house, the magnetic sympathy of the audience, the impassive attention of the jury, and the dramatic suspense of the moment. It is the capacity to turn all these things to account that produces forensic eloquence. Herndon describes a triumph of Lincoln on behalf of the widow of a revolutionary soldier. The defendant was a rascally agent who had pocketed half her pension by way of fee. The whole speech was a very eloquent appeal, and the final words to the jury, if you read them aloud that they may catch the ear, have the ring of sound advocacy in them: "Time rolls by; the heroes of 'seventy-six' have passed away and are encamped on the other shore. The soldier has gone to rest; and now, crippled, blinded, and broken, his widow comes to you and to me, gentlemen of the jury, to right her wrongs. She was not always thus. She was once a beautiful woman. Her step was as elastic, her face as fair and her voice as sweet, as any that rang in the mountains of old Virginia. But now she is poor and defenceless out here on the prairies of Illinois, many hundreds of miles away from the scenes of her childhood. She appeals to us who enjoy the privileges achieved for us by the patriots of the Revolution for our sympathetic aid and manly protection. All I ask is, Shall we befriend her?"

The poor old lady obtained judgment, Lincoln paid her hotel bill, and sent her home rejoicing and free of all expense. The notes from which he spoke give us an interesting peep behind the scenes into the machinery of advocacy. They run thus: "No contract—money obtained by Defendant not given by Plaintiff—Revolutionary War—Describe Valley Forge privations—Ice—Soldier's bleeding feet—Plaintiff's husband, soldier leaving home for army—Skin Defendant! Close!" As a delighted contemporary remarked: "When Abe set out to skin a defendant it was some!"

Although he did not rise to the extraordinary heights of vituperation to which O'Connell soared, he was a dangerous man to insult. Forquer, once a Whig, but then a Democrat and office-holder, built himself the finest house in Springfield and decorated it with the first lightning-rod that had ever been seen in the county. He had been abusing Lincoln as a young man who wanted taking down, and when Lincoln's turn came he appealed to the audience: "It is for you, not for me, to say whether I am up or down. This gentleman has alluded to my being a young man. I am older in years than I am in the tricks and trades of politicians. I desire to live, and I desire place and distinction as a politician, but I would rather die now than like this gentleman live to see the day when I should have to erect a lightning-rod to protect a guilty conscience from an offended God."

He never talked over the heads of the jury. He led them along with him. He was lucid and fair in statement and his skill lay in "conducting a common mind along the chain of his logic to his own conclusion." He grasped the great essential in advocacy, that you must not only know the real point of your own case, but that as a rule it lies in a very narrow compass, and that your main duty is not to lose sight of it yourself and never let the Court and jury get away from it. A new generation wanting to know by what trick Lincoln gained so many verdicts was enlightened by an old colleague who replied, "He instinctively saw the kernel of every case at the outset, never lost sight of it, and never let it escape the jury." That, he said triumphantly, "was the only trick I ever saw him play." His powers of homely humorous illustrations often set the courts in a roar. When Lincoln's eye twinkled and he drawled out, "That reminds me," a chuckle of approbation ran through the Court-house as when a favourite comedian steps upon the stage. It is impossible to reproduce these stories effectively in print, but as good an instance as any is the following yarn by which he illustrated his client's point of view in an assault case.

"It reminds me," he said, "of the man who was attacked by a furious dog, which he killed with a pitchfork."

" What made you kill my dog ? " demanded the farmer.

" What made him try to bite me ? " retorted the offender.

" But why didn't you go at him with the other end of your pitchfork ? " persisted the farmer.

" Well, why didn't he come at me with his other end ? "

Again, speaking to a jury on the preponderance of evidence, and trying to explain to them what a lawyer means by the phrase, " weight of evidence," he laid down the legal principle in these words : " If you were going to bet on this case, on which side would you be willing to risk a ' fippenny ' ? That side upon which you would be willing to bet a ' fippenny ' is the side on which rests the preponderance of evidence in your minds. It is possible that you may not be right, but that is not the question. The question is as to where the preponderance of evidence lies, and you can judge exactly where it lies in your minds by deciding as to which side you would be willing to bet on." A man who could talk horse sense after that fashion in a law court would be listened to in attentive sympathy by any twelve English-speaking men gathered together in the right box.

The circumstances under which his career as an advocate came to an end are part of a greater story. In June of 1860 Lincoln was waiting with his friends in a newspaper office at Springfield when the news flashed through from Chicago : " The Convention has made a nomination and Seward is—the second man on the list." Lincoln cut short his friends' congratulations and pocketed the telegram, saying, " There is a little woman on Eighth Street who would like to hear about this."

What the Judge Thought

When the Presidential Election was over and he had to leave Springfield for Washington, he came into his office and spent some hours with his friend and partner " Billy " Herndon, settling things up. After the business was done, he threw himself on to the old horsehair sofa and, gazing up at the ceiling in his favourite attitude when he was thinking out a law case, said with a sigh, " Billy, how long have we been together ? "

" Over sixteen years," said his friend.

" We've never had a cross word during all that time, have we ? "

" No, indeed we have not."

He lay in thought for a few minutes, and then rose and gathered up a bundle of papers and books. As he said good-bye to " Billy " his eye caught the old signboard which hung on its rusty hinges at the foot of the stairway. " I want that to remain," he said in a low voice. " Let it hang there undisturbed. Give our clients to understand that the election of a President makes no change in the firm of ' Lincoln and Herndon.' If I live I'm coming back some time, and then we'll go right on practising law as if nothing had ever happened."

What did happen is written in the history of the world. One can scarcely believe that Lincoln himself ever expected to return and ride the Illinois circuit and sit in the Springfield office again. But he loved his profession, and he knew that his fellow-lawyers honoured and respected him. As long as the old sign hung on the stairway the President of the United States was still Abraham Lincoln, advocate.

Chapter II: *Concerning the Law of the Lost Golf Ball*

THE law of the lost golf ball is a serious subject far too wide to be adequately treated in a few paragraphs. But amid much hasty generalisation of ready writers it may be well at least to set out the lines upon which scientific research should proceed.

There are many kinds of law relating to the lost golf ball; there is the law of dynamics by which it is or should be hit, the law of nature by which it is sliced or pulled, the law of chance by which your opponent lays his dead, and the penal law of the Royal and Ancient Golf Club of St. Andrews which provides appropriate punishment for the misdemeanour of losing a ball. These subjects are of themselves worthy of volumes written by appropriate professors, nor should I dare to venture a word upon them. My humble task is merely to state in non-technical language as far as possible the status of the golf ball at common law, with special reference to the difficult questions concerning the rights of property in a lost ball and the consideration of the extent to which it may be the subject matter of larceny. I recognise that when the great final volume on the Law of the Golf Ball is written by some ponderous German or elegant English jurist, there will be chapters on the Commercial Law of the Golf Ball, the Patent Law in relation to the same, the golf ball in Chancery will have to be treated of at length, and the legal incidents of its career in relation to Probate, Admiralty, and even Divorce will give rise to many brilliant chapters of equal length and learning.

Nor do I propose to say much about the civil law of the golf ball. I am going to assume that there is such a thing as property in a golf ball. A golf ball, I take it, is the subject of ownership, although the ownership is of a very fleeting and precarious nature. There was a school of legal thought in the fourteenth century that considered golf balls to be *feræ naturæ*—that is to say, akin to beasts and birds that are wild, such as hares, foxes, wild geese, and the like, wherein no man may claim a property. The germ of the idea is said to be found in the writings of Grotius, who noticed that often the flight of the golf ball was like that of the hare along the ground, that on occasion after the manner of foxes it hid itself in inaccessible holes, and that it was stuffed with the feathers of wild geese. By what later writers considered a false analogy, the early jurists considered a golf ball to have so many of the qualities of *feræ naturæ* and to be so little subject to the dominion of man, that there could be no property in it in a scientific legal sense, although you might have casual possession of it before you struck it from the tee. This is really a matter of historical jurisprudence into the maze of which it is well not to wander. Remember, moreover, that Grotius was a Dutchman—the motto of the Grotius family was " Bunkert Dam "—most Dutchmen of his date were golfers, and nothing is more misleading in these questions than to let your judgment be obscured by your experiences of the game. For the purposes of this essay, therefore, I ask you to set aside your natural instincts and experiences and assume that a golf ball is a chattel in which there can be property and over which it is possible for the owner to exercise dominion.

There seems to be no doubt, then, that if a man lose a golf ball and another find it, the original owner can have an action of Trover and Conversion against the finder. This is very ancient law, that where one man gets possession of the goods of another by finding—hence our law term " trover " (trouver)—or otherwise, and refuses to deliver them to the owner, or sells or converts them to his own use without the consent of the owner, the owner can recover the value of his goods.

But from a business point of view it is a privilege of very little worth. Let us put a case. A. drives into the rough at the fourteenth and loses his ball—a new Baby Chestnut. B. three days afterwards finds a ball in the rough at the fourteenth and refuses to show it to A., but admits in the club house to several members that it is a Baby Chestnut. A. puts the matter into the hands of his solicitor, who collects from the club members the evidence of the statements made by B. and advises A. that he can maintain trover. A plaint is issued in the County Court, price one shilling, claiming two shillings and sixpence or the return of a new Baby Chestnut, the property of the Plaintiff, wrongfully converted to his own use by the Defendant. The Defendant pays sixpence into Court, denying liability. This subterfuge is a kind of legal stymie much in vogue among railway companies, corporations, and other non-sportsmanlike bodies. A. refusing to accept B.'s gambit of the proffered sixpence, now gives B. notice to produce the golf ball at the hearing of the case. At the day of trial the hearing fee, price two shillings, being paid, the solicitors on each side duly briefed—price, say, £1 1s. each—the case is called on. The ball is produced and is certainly a Baby Chestnut, but not a new Baby Chestnut. A., however, admits paternity and swears it is the ball he lost. B.'s solicitor points out that the ball has a bad cut on its starboard cheek and the paint is knocked off where it has recently collided with a tree, that if A. had mentioned these descriptive defects, which must have been within his knowledge, B. would have delivered up the golf ball, and that in any case the sixpence paid into Court is greatly in excess of the value of the ball produced.

The learned Judge, after viewing the golf ball and consulting the Registrar—who having more leisure and money than the Judge is usually of a lower handicap—decides that the ball is not worth twopence. He allows the Plaintiff, however, to take twopence out of court, the remaining fourpence to be returned to the Defendant, and as the Plaintiff could have taken out the sixpence when it was paid in, he orders the Plaintiff to pay the Defendant's costs as from that date. These he allows on a higher scale, with a certificate under Section 119 that the case is of importance to a certain class of the community, to wit, golfers. Of course, each case would be tried out upon its merits, but personally I cannot see how an endeavour to maintain "trover" for a lost golf ball can ever be a business proposition for anyone but the solicitor who advises the action, his fellow-solicitor who defends it, and the Treasury who pockets the fees for the trial. But this is not only true of actions about golf balls, but is really a common incident of actions at law in general.

Of course, if A. could have locked up B. for a month for the theft of his golf ball, A.—whom I do not regard as a true sport—would have had the chuckle over B. And it is really this subject of the larceny of a lost golf ball that drew me into the meshes of research. Would that I had leisure hours and genius worthy of the task, for I have indeed discovered a deep mine of legal learning, though I have only time roughly to stake out the claim.

The first point that I break the shins of my ignorance upon is what law am I to apply? This is a question for the international lawyer, for the antiquary, and the dry-as-dust pundit who revel in these matters. We know for certain that golf was a very ancient Scots game. As early as the fifteenth century we find references to "fute-ball, golfe, or uther sik unprofitabill sportis" in Scots Acts of Parliament. James I of England and VI of Scotland in a letter dated Salisbury, August 5, 1618, noting that no small quantity of gold and silver is leaving Scotland for buying of golf balls, confers a monopoly of ball-manufacture on James Melvill of Edinburgh for the space of twenty-one years. Each ball was not to exceed in price four shillings, and Melvill was ordained to have "ane particular stamp of his awin and that all ballis maid within the kingdome found to be uther wayis stampit sall be escheated." In plain English, any other ball but the genuine " red spot Melvill " found its way into the royal golf bag by forfeiture or escheat. And as James and his son Henry were regular players at Blackheath, this regal experiment in tariff reform was of considerable advantage to both of them.

But the value of the story to us is that it raises doubt in the legal mind whether an Englishman has any rights at all as against a Scotsman in the matter of golf balls. Clearly in James I's day—and let us remember that as Defender of the Faith whatever he did or said is worthy of all regard—an Englishman could not make a golf ball or have any property in one unless it was one of Melvill's. The point at once occurs—to one who is bound to admit that he has never opened an international law book since he endeavoured to pass an examination on the subject—is the theft of a golf ball to be decided by the domicil of the golf ball or the *lex loci* of the links? Supposing for instance, A. in 1620 lost a four-bob Melvill at Blackheath and a caddie was found in possession of it, what law should Justice Shallow apply—the Scots law of " theft " or the English law of " larceny "? Because if the *lex loci*, or the law of the links, is to prevail in each place where golf is played, we may have to study the Code Napoléon at Le Touquet, the statutes of the Jurats at Grouville, and the ancient laws of Hywel Dda when we venture on the Morfa within the jurisdiction of Harlech.

I mention these difficulties, not to solve them, but to show you how stupendous are the legal problems raised by the lost golf ball. In this country it will, I expect, be decided either that the royal and ancient game carries with it—as it seems to have done in James I's time—all the incidents and privileges of Scots Law, or else perhaps modern doctrines will be followed and the felonious taking of a lost golf ball will be dealt with under English statutes.

We may leave it at this until the Court of Criminal Appeal gets seisin of the subject, thankful that there are but few minor distinctions between Scots theft and English larceny. The practical question, I take it, that is burdening the mind of the golfer who loses his ball in the rough, and the loafer who prowls round the links in company of a trained lurcher with a gutty nose, is what are the sporting chances of seven days without the option?

Now, in the Jacobean days of golf it seems to have been clear law in the Criminal Courts that finding was keeping. Sir Edward Coke's view—and he was James I's Chief Justice—was that "if one lose his own goods and another find them, though he convert them *animo furandi* to his own use, yet it is no larceny, for the first taking is lawful. So if one find Treasure Trove or waife or straie and convert them *ut supra*, it is no larceny both in respect of the finding and also for that *Dominus non apparet.*"

I like to study these old lawyers, they put their case with such subtle common sense. Dominus in 1620 slices into the rough from the third tee at Blackheath and after prolonged search abandons his four-shilling Melvill. Two days afterwards Bardolph on his way to Gadshill, crossing the heath, picks up the Melvill and keeps it. This is no larceny, for Dominus has gone back to Whitehall and *non apparet*. If, however, our friend Bardolf had seen

Dominus slice into the rough and had marked the ball down and gone for it at the moment when the back of Dominus was turned, that would have been a very different matter, I presume. The law, however, was not eager to extend the incidents of larceny, since on conviction for the theft of a Melvill, if the jury found it to be of the value of over one shilling, that was grand larceny and the penalty was death.

And Sir Matthew Hale points out a very sensible exception to the old rule of law that " finding is keeping." For he tells us that " where a man's goods are in such a place where ordinarily they are or may be placed, and a person takes them *animo furandi*, it is felony, and the pretence of finding must not excuse." For instance, I know a certain under-sheriff of whom at the third hole it might fairly be recorded that his drives, in the words of Hale, " ordinarily are or may be placed " in the zariba. A zariba with us is gorse and trees surrounded by a thin ditch and out of bounds. I refer to my friend as a certain under-sheriff not to identify him, but because he is certain or nearly certain to drive into the zariba. If, then, a ball be found in that particular zariba it would, I think, come within the rule " where a man's goods are in such a place where ordinarily they are or may be placed," and it would be larceny for anyone to take them *animo furandi*. And let the layman remember that without the *animus* and intent to steal mere asportation is no crime whatsoever. And that the Scots Law is in no way different from the English Law as laid down in Sir Matthew Hale's *Historia Placitorum Coronæ* may be seen by the study of the works of the famous Baron Hume, a noted writer of commentaries on Scots Criminal Law. As late as 1797 the learned Baron tells us that for a cabman to appropriate a parcel in his cab was not theft. There is no doubt that the principle of "finding is keeping" had the sanction of the old lawyers.

It seems clear, therefore, that up to the beginning of the nineteenth century if you found a derelict golf ball you might pocket it and play with it without fear of the police; the only remedy of the owner, if it came to his ears that you had found his ball, being an action in Trover and Conversion, with a remote hope of recovering damages. But as the penalty for theft became less severe, so the standard of honesty set by the law of larceny has been gradually raised, and to-day the old rule "finding is keeping" is no longer a part of the common law of England or even of Scotland, where we know they keep the Sabbath and everything else they can lay their hands on. The rule to-day, and a very sensible and practical rule it is, seems to be this: "If a man finds goods that have been actually lost or are reasonably supposed by him to have been lost, and appropriates them with intent to take the entire dominion over them, really believing when he takes them that the owner cannot be found, it is *not* larceny; but if he takes them with the like intent though lost, or reasonably believing that the owner can be found, it *is* larceny."

Thus if my caddie, knowing that I have lost a ball in the hedgerow at the tenth, goes back in the evening and finds it, well knowing by the gaping wound at the base of it—this was caused by the low tee he gave me at the seventh, and he cannot have forgotten the shot—if,

I say, he takes the ball with intent to exercise entire dominion over it, as, for instance, to exchange it for cigarettes or sell it, that is larceny. But if, say, with full intent to return it to me the next morning, he plays a round with it himself in the dusk of the evening and loses it in the pond, he is not guilty of larceny, and my only remedy is an action for damages. For it is no answer when I sue the caddie in detinue for him to say that he has abandoned possession of my golf ball; on the contrary, it is all the worse for him, for the Judge would remember the maxim *omnia praesumunter contra spoliatorem*, and he would refer the jury to the famous case of the chimney-sweep who found a jewel and gave it to a jeweller to value, who refused to return it, whereon it was laid down that " unless the Defendant did produce the jewel and show it not to be of the finest water they should presume the strongest against him and make the value of the best jewels the measure of their damage." And the law of golf balls is the same as the law of jewels, since, as Thomas Spens the Younger of Lathallan used to say in the days of the feather ball, " A guid ba' is a jewel."

But you are to observe that if you prosecute your caddie for larceny, it is up to you—if the boy be under fourteen—to prove that he was a lad of guile with sufficient intelligence to appreciate that the old law of " finding is keeping " has been improved off the face of the bench, and that other considerations prevail. For the humane and sensible common law of this country, as Hale tells us, is that " an infant under the age of discretion regularly cannot be guilty of larceny, viz. under fourteen years, unless it appears by circumstances that he hath a discretion more than the law presumes." An infant under seven is incapable of crime, and between seven and fourteen is presumably incapable of crime unless there is evidence to show that he possesses the degree of knowledge and intelligence equivalent to that of an adult criminal. This sane and ancient law seems sometimes overlooked by country magistrates dealing with the children of the poor, but I feel sure that no true golfer would wish an apparently larcenous boy of thirteen to receive even four strokes, unless such handicap was really his due under the common law.

And there is a disconcerting phrase in the Commentaries of Baron Hume that—were it popularly known—might tempt many to dishonesty. "The abstraction of a dead body," he writes, "is not theft." From this it has been hastily assumed by some that anybody's ball lying really dead might be stolen with impunity. But a learned Writer to the Signet has explained to me that though a body lying dead—as even my approach shot has been known to do on occasions—is not the subject of larceny, yet as soon as the dishonest person lifts the ball it ceases to be dead, and that little fact of asportation, or as my Scots friends say, *a-motio*, sets going the whole machinery of the criminal law against the felonious one. And though I receive his opinion with every respect, yet until the dead golf ball has been adjudicated upon by the Courts it must, I think, be open to doubt whether or not—being undoubtedly a dead body—it is the subject of larceny.

And of the golf ball washed up on the sea-shore and

found as you take your Sunday stroll upon the beach very different considerations prevail. Such a golf ball I take to be a Wreck de Mer, being undoubtedly in the last instance *ejectum maris*. Personally, the kind of ball that I tee up at the tenth at Llandudno or the sixth at Newquay, or at any seaside hole, is a wreck before it starts, but once driven the shipwreck is generally complete. And when such goods are cast upon the land by the sea and left there within some county, it seems that they belong to the King by his prerogative as Lord of the Narrow Seas, or perhaps to the Lord of the Manor. And remember that your golf ball may be either *flotsam*, *jetsam*, or *ligan*. *Flotsam* if it is a floater and remains on the surface, *jetsam* if it sinks and remains under water, *ligan* if you know where it is lying and have marked it with a buoy. My experience is that the boy very seldom marks it. But in all these cases if you do not appear to claim your ball it is the King's—unless he hath made a grant of wreck *jetsam*, *flotsam* and *ligan*, to the Lord of the Manor. The penalties that may be suffered by one who picks up a golf ball on the foreshore and thereby interferes with rights of " Wreck " are very serious, but the mere statement of law that in so doing one may be tampering with the royal prerogative will be sufficient to restrain the true golfer from so disloyal an action.

As to retrieving one's own ball immediately from the sea, that I think is permissible since if the owner claimed his goods within three months it is on record that even a monarch of the tendencies of Richard III did not seek to insist upon his franchise of Wreck. And of the unfortunate who pulls into the sea—it is usually a pull except at North Berwick, where you slice—it would, I think, be held as of other shipwrecked mortals *omnes res suas liberas et quietas haberet*, so that if he can retrieve his wrecked chattel he may have it, or if he is drowned in the endeavour to save it his children may have it, or his brothers or sisters, but in default of these it is the King's. And though I can find no direct authority upon the point, yet my legal instinct leads me to believe that this law of Wreck only applies to the sea and tidal waters; and that in respect of inland lakes, tarns, rivers, streams, ponds, and casual water in bunkers, there is no danger of interfering with His Majesty's prerogative by reclaiming your ball when you are lucky enough to find it *flotsam* and not *jetsam*.

It was this consideration of the law of Wreck in its relation to the lost golf ball at sea that led me to the perception of what I believe to be the true rule of law as to the lost golf ball on land. I can foresee that I shall gain little credit for this discovery. Some will say it is merely the perception of the obvious and has always been known to be sound law by scientific jurists; others will simply deny that there is any legal sense in the theory at all. For myself, deep as my research into the matter has been, at present I only put forth the idea tentatively, as a legal theory worthy of examination by those professors and pundits whose leisure and salaries enable them to deal with law as a pure science uncontaminated by any human interests whatever.

Shortly, the notion is this. I believe that a lost golf ball, by which I mean "lost" within the meaning of the code of law of the Royal and Ancient, and abandoned by the Dominus of the ball, who gives up all hope of future possession of it—such a golf ball is, I maintain, when it is discovered again, in the eyes of the law, Treasure Trove, *Thesaurus inventus*, and subject to all the legal incidents thereof. For when you place a new half-crown Spotted Tangent down a rabbit-hole, what are you doing but depositing treasure in the earth and hiding it in some private place? When it is found again is it not, as old Bracton says, *vetus depositio pecuniae?* For if it be objected that Treasure Trove must be either gold or silver, that is, I opine, too narrow a definition, for we know that plate and bullion have always been considered Treasure Trove. And it will remain for the Judges to decide whether they consider a golf ball comes within the direct meaning of the word "bullion," tracing it through the French *boulon* and giving it its original meaning of ball; or whether, as modern Judges sometimes do, they will throw aside their modest ignorance of daily affairs and take judicial notice of the extravagant cost of golf balls, and decide that the finding of a new Spotted Tangent is in law the same thing as the finding of half a crown. If either of these views be taken—and surely one or other is sound, if not both—then it must follow that a lost golf ball is in law—as it is in fact—hidden treasure abandoned by the true owner. In early times Bracton tells us that Treasure Trove belonged to the finder, but now all hidden treasure, whether casually lost and unclaimed or designedly abandoned, is, according to Grotius, the property of the King. If I am right, then it is the duty of every loyal subject on finding a golf ball to make it known to the Coroner of the county who acts for the

King in these matters; and should the Coroner hear of any finds of lost golf balls in his diocese, it is clearly his duty to hold an inquest on them and to discover and hand over to justice the finders. For, remember, to discover Treasure Trove and to conceal the discovery from the King's bailiff has always been a grave offence, being in early times punishable by death and to-day by grievous fine and imprisonment.

For myself I shall run no risks, and the next golf ball I find I shall forward to our County Coroner with a petition that the Crown will be pleased to allow me the costs and expense to which I have been put in recovering and forwarding the Treasure Trove. We shall then be able to discover by a practical test the views of our rulers upon this important subject.

Another complicated question that must, one would think, find its way into the Courts before long is what is the legal position of A. and B. being partners in a foursome? A. loses B.'s ball. This raises the much larger question—What is a foursome? You speak of your colleague in a foursome as a partner, but the mere fact of playing for a ball a corner, and thereby sharing the assets or liabilities of the afternoon, does not, I suggest, create a true partnership. A foursome is probably only a joint adventure.

Suppose A. tees up a new red-spot Dormouse and drives it successfully up the fairway. B. now plays the second and punches the ball into the bracken and it is lost. Has A. any remedy against B.? A. will say that he directed B. to play to the left of the pin and that the shot into the bracken was an unauthorised act permanently depriving him of his property and that this amounts to conversion. B., on the other hand, will contend that it was " an accident arising out of and in the course of " the joint adventure. As to what this phrase means, although I have read all that the Court of Appeal has said about it during the last twenty years, I would not venture to express any opinion of my own ; but in any litigation that ensued between A. and B. my money would be on B. if he was prepared to take the case to the House of Lords.

But if A. and B. differ in sex and the match is what is called a " mixed " foursome, there are some who think that since the Sex Disqualification (Removal) Act the law of the lost golf ball is the same as in a man's foursome and that nowadays a foursome cannot legally be " mixed." Clearly this would not be so if A. happens to be a peeress in her own right. But, in any case, if your lady partner puts down a repainted Colonel and you, in Freud's phrase, " push it into the unconscious," your privilege at the end of the day is clearly to offer her a new Dormouse. And this is so not under the Common Law but under the Law of Chivalry, and you will find it set out in the *fabliaux*.

As I said in the beginning so I now repeat. This question is all too large and intricate for one mind, and all I have attempted here is to note down the headings for future discussion. Whether the matter should be handed over to a Royal or Departmental Commission is for others to decide. For my own part I should suggest a permanent Historical and Legal Commission of Scots and English lawyers and antiquarians. They might co-opt a few long handicap Cabinet Ministers who I understand are constant contributors to that form of Treasure Trove known as the lost golf ball. Considering the large but as yet unascertained value of this continually increasing deposit of treasure, it is to be hoped in the interests of the State that something will be done to settle these vexed questions of private and public rights to which I have called attention and recover for the community any increment that is theirs.

Chapter III: *Concerning Legal Out-Patients*

THE cost of litigation to poor people and the avarice of lawyers are themes upon which social reformers in all ages have waxed righteously indignant. Piers Plowman pictured the Serjeants-at-law of his day: " Pleading the law for pennies and for pounds ; Unlocking their lips never for love of our Lord." Dickens chastised us with the grim drama of the Chancery prisoner in the Fleet and the unlucky cobbler who successfully defended his title to a fortune and was imprisoned for life by his lawyers on account of costs.

Even Thackeray, who cared for none of these things, allowed Policeman X. to burst out into a ballad of indignation about the costs in the " Pallis Court " where poor Jacob Homnium was cruelly bled.

" The debt was two seventeen
(Which he no more owed than you),
And then there was the plaintive's costs.
Eleven pound six and two.

And then there was his own,
Which the lawyers they did fix
At the wery modderit figgur
Of ten pound one and six."

And though we may have got rid of some of the more scandalous cruelties of this form of injustice and to some extent tempered the wind of costs to the shorn litigant, yet the poor man to-day who enters a Court of Justice to obtain or defend his rights comes out at the end of it all not perhaps as fully fleeced as poor Jacob was, but neatly clipped and trimmed of much superfluous wool.

The scandal of the high cost of litigation in this country has attracted the attention of even the Judges on the Bench. The waste of litigation is indeed a terrible burden on the poor. For every sovereign recovered by means of a County Court you may reckon that something like ten shillings has to be spent in costs and fees. The lawyer is blamed somewhat unfairly for this condition of things, and lawyers are perhaps as unpopular a class to-day as they were in the time of Piers Plowman.

One may say that all professions meet with abuse in these crazy times and that the lawyer shares the satire of his generation with the priest and the doctor. But this is not the whole truth of the matter. You may meet in fiction—or even in real life—with a priest or a doctor who is the beloved hero of all who come in contact with him, but a lawyer never. Nor is the reason far to seek. The legal profession has its high ideals, but the practitioner is too modest to call attention to them, and is apt to concentrate on his privileges rather than his duties and to use these for personal advancement rather than public service. The Bar Council and the Solicitors' Society will meet and discuss their duty to Mammon, but their duty to their neighbour is a subject that is taboo. The instinct of self-preservation should lead to a more generous attitude in matters of legal reform. We live in a world of revolutionary changes, and many good and valuable machines may be readily scrapped merely because they are put to unworthy and selfish purposes when they might be employed for the public weal. There never was an age in which it was more necessary for old-fashioned institutions to examine their charters, consider their credentials, and ask themselves without bias whether the work they are doing justifies them in asking for a place in the sun of the new world.

Consider and compare for a moment the different conduct of the legal and medical professions towards the poor in the matter of gratuitous assistance. What splendid services are rendered by the doctors! What is done by the lawyers? At every great hospital doctors of the highest eminence in their profession give voluntary assistance to whomsoever is in need of their help. Why should not there be legal hospitals or, at all events, out-patient departments in every city in the country? Something of the kind, no doubt, exists, but it is as yet but poorly organised and badly equipped. What would be more likely to endear lawyers to the hearts of the people than to see a Simon or a Marshall Hall in a crowded room in the Borough studying the legal ailments of the patients of the district, prescribing affidavits and interrogatories for their cure and lecturing to a band of devoted students how justice might be administered to these poor persons.

That such an idea should sound strange and even ludicrous to modern ears shows how far we have strayed and erred from the higher paths of legal duty. From the dawn of Anglo-Saxon legal history we have at least murmured with our lips that justice was to be done alike to rich and poor. The idea was embodied in that paragraph of Magna Carta which is one of our great historical traditions: "To no one will we sell, to no one will we refuse or delay right or justice." In theory, justice is free to all, but can we honestly say that our practice of the law to-day does not in fact refuse and delay justice to poor people?

To those who hold as I do the belief that advocacy is essential to the right administration of justice, it follows as a matter of course that the services of an advocate must be accessible to all who require them. The legal profession will find it hard to justify its position in the eyes of a new generation if it neglects its primary duty of giving counsel to the ignorant and defending the weak and the oppressed.

In the State of Washington the final clause of the oath of admission to the Bar ends thus: "I will never reject from any consideration personal to myself the cause of the defenceless or the oppressed or delay any man's cause for lucre or malice, so help me God." This is merely a corollary to Magna Carta, and though we have never set it down in writing we may accept it, I think, as part of the unwritten code of honour by which our own professional life is governed. And if lawyers forget their oath in this matter and fail to co-operate with doctors and priests in the service of the poor, a time will come when our profession will be in danger of judgment, after which there will be no long stay of execution.

Lord Brougham was the great apostle of the duty of lawyers to the poor, and a hundred years ago he warned us of our neglect and pointed out the narrow way of reform, but his gospel fell on deaf ears. To-day there is perhaps a small revival, and now, both here and in America, the cause of Justice and the Poor may be preached without neglect to increasing congregations.

Ex-President Taft, in speaking a few years ago to the Virginia Bar of the importance of the improvement of the administration of justice, said: "We must make it so that the poor man will have as nearly as possible an equal opportunity in litigating as the rich man, and under present conditions, ashamed as we may be of it, this is not the fact." His recent visit to England was made for the express purpose of studying our system and seeing if we had remedies for that disease of delay which so notably affects American litigation. We are joint-heirs with the United States of the principles laid down in Magna Carta and can study each other's efforts towards right action with sympathy and hope of reforms.

Much good work is being done in the United States in the matter of legal out-patients, and those who wish to go into the detail of the matter may be commended to the pages of "Justice and the Poor," by Reginald Heber Smith, of the Boston Bar. The arrangements of the assignment of counsel to poor litigants and the system of providing an advocate for poor criminals, like our own recent experiments of a similar character, fall very short of Chief Justice Taft's ideal of equality. More seems to have been done in America than we have hitherto attempted in the way of giving free legal advice, but it is noticeable that the work is largely carried out by charitable societies and citizens unconnected with the Bar, though individual lawyers with an instinct for charity freely give their services to these societies as they do with us.

But the traditional duty of the profession to place its services at the disposal of the poor without fee or reward is in the United States, as it is in England, more honoured in the breach than the observance. And until we find some leading member of the Bar preaching a crusade to his brethren and the outer world for a revival of the ancient rights of the poor to have their writs for nothing, to be freed from costs and to have counsels and attorneys to aid them—in a word, until lawyers carry out these primary duties to the poor, which are the real basis of their privileges, so long shall we be justifying the platform utterances about lawyers of Jack Cade and Dick the Butcher.

If the profession would interest itself in a practical way by supplying the free services of a trained advocate where that is essential to the administration of justice, it would do much to convince an unbelieving world in the eternal mission of the lawyer. A movement by lawyers to free the law from its staggering burden of costs and fees would go far to satisfy the public of the good faith of the profession.

As we long ago abolished turn-pike tolls on the King's highway, so should we pull down the old barriers and open the King's Courts of Justice free to all citizens. The taking of fees and the payment of officials by fees—where it still obtains—are relics of barbarism. The essential service of justice, like education, highways, police, drainage, gas and water in public places, parks and libraries, should be a free service, and when at long last it is made a free service the generation which looks back on our own schedules of fees and bills of costs will regard us with contempt and amazement.

When the State and the lawyers and the public generally recognise the essential necessity of the freedom of justice and begin to take steps towards practical reform, they will discover that the bulk of litigation that takes place is not only grossly wasteful of wealth, but destructive to human peace of mind. At the present stage of civilisation it would be premature to suggest that litigation could be abolished altogether, but the bulk of it is unnecessary and harmful and could easily be dispensed with. In the eighteenth century the doctors used to bleed all their patients, and lawyers to-day are inclined to prescribe the bleeding treatment of litigation for all their patients' woes. A really sane lawyer would propose the more modern treatment of conciliation, but it is curious how suspicious the patient himself is of this new-fangled cure and how he clings to the old-fashioned remedy of bleeding which he and his fathers have undergone for generations.

It is a sad thing that whilst other countries have instituted Courts of Conciliation, England has never made the smallest experiment in this direction, so that if St. Paul were to land upon our shores to-day he might ask the same question he put to the Corinthians: "Is it so that there cannot be found among you one wise man who shall be able to decide between his brethren?"

Lord Brougham made proposals for the formation of Conciliation Courts and pointed out how much money and temper might be saved if, as a condition precedent to litigation, disputants were bound to meet in the presence of a trained and impartial third person holding the dignity of judicial office who could exhibit to them the pitfalls of litigation and the advantages of a just and peaceful settlement. Note that this must take place in the early stages of the quarrel. The parties must come to the judge by themselves without lawyers and the business of the conciliator will not be to judge the merits of the case, but to explore the avenues of peace and see if there is any honourable alternative to litigation. If no conciliation is possible, then the judge will mark the case "fit for litigation," and the case will proceed as at present.

During the recent visit of the Danish judges and lawyers to England I had the privilege of discussing this matter with them, and the success of the system as practised in Denmark seems beyond dispute. Lord Brougham called our attention to the Conciliation Courts of Denmark, which have existed since 1795. These courts have jurisdiction in every civil proceeding, and it is a condition precedent to litigation that the dispute should be submitted to a Conciliation Court.

As in our own country there are different procedures in our High Courts and County Courts, so in Denmark the methods of Conciliation Courts are somewhat different in those courts which administer justice in Copenhagen and those which administer justice outside Copenhagen. In the same way, we find the procedure within Copenhagen is simpler in the Town Court where small cases are heard than in the High Court.

It will be sufficient to describe shortly the methods of conciliation which obtain in the High Court of Justice in

Copenhagen, for the details of which I am beholden to Mr. Ostenfeld, of the Danish Bar. The principle of 1795 that conciliation must be attempted before litigation ensues stands good in the High Court. The Special Court of Conciliation of the High Court consists of three members, a magistrate, i.e. a mayor or alderman, a town councillor and a member appointed by the Ministry of Justice. Prior to 1916 the last member was always a High Court judge, but now he must be a layman, so that the whole tribunal is non-judicial.

In Copenhagen the plaintiff and defendant need not appear personally, as they are bound to do in the country districts, but may appear by counsel or any one authorised by power of attorney. The cases are always heard in camera, and everything said or done is without prejudice to any litigation that may ensue. If as the result of a conciliation a defendant admits a debt, for instance, and agrees to pay by instalments, this agreement is entered, so that it has the effect of a judgment.

There are a few causes of action to which the principle that conciliation is a condition precedent to litigation does not apply. If, for instance, the defendant puts in a counter-claim, or where the action is on a bill of exchange, or where the action is against the supreme power of the State, or the matter is considered urgent—these are some of the circumstances to which conciliation is neither necessary or appropriate.

That the system is a very valuable one cannot be denied, and that it leads to big results in money economy and human reconciliation is beyond doubt. Heber Smith tells us that in Norway 75 per cent and in Denmark 90 per cent of all litigation is peaceably adjusted through judicial conciliation. Precise figures for the Norwegian Courts in 1888 are known. The total number of civil cases brought was 103,969, of which 2300 were dismissed by the Conciliation Commissioner. Of the remaining 101,669, conciliation produced adjustments agreeable to the litigants in 81,015 cases, and in addition 7886 were submitted to the Conciliation Court by the parties for decision. Thus only 12,768 cases went to the regular Courts for formal litigation, this informal preliminary tribunal of conciliation having disposed of 87 per cent of all matters to the satisfaction of both parties.

Statistics are dull, unhandsome reading, but translate these figures into human units and consider how much anxiety and worry has been saved to the thousands of human beings interested in these affairs. Not only is the saving of their money and time of value to the citizens and to the community of whom they are units, but you must also give credit for that nobler economy in hatred, malice, and all uncharitableness that is the worst form of waste in a lawsuit and clogs the wheels of human relationship for so many years after the decision and the event.

And it is not only in Scandinavian countries that Conciliation Courts are endemic. They are to be found in a different form in both Italy and France. In the latter country it has long been the duty of the *juge de paix* to bring disputants together and endeavour to persuade them to bury the hatchet and live in neighbourly peace, and those who have had experience of the French practice speak highly of its social convenience.

So that instead of regarding ourselves with complacent insular satisfaction in this matter of Conciliation Courts we should rather begin to think furiously whether there is not a blot on our legal scutcheon which might be wiped away and whether we might not learn from our neighbours new lessons about justice and the poor.

English-speaking people move slowly, and though lawyers and publicists have had the virtues of Conciliation Courts before their eyes since Lord Brougham called attention to them a hundred years ago, yet it is difficult to get either laymen or lawyers to discuss them seriously. One reason is, no doubt, that lawyers who can best appreciate their value are not in this country—or perhaps in any other—ardent upholders of reforms that may cut down fees. The man in the street, too, who is most vocally abusive about the attorney, when he reads of a scheme for his elimination, is suddenly conscience-stricken and murmurs to himself that, bad as he is, the attorney, after all, is a man and a brother.

But it is not the elimination of the attorney that is sought after, but rather that the attorney should be put to higher uses and allowed to earn a living by some more honourable pursuit than that of exchanging useless letters with another of his kind, in the blessed hope that in the litigation they are promoting the costs of their futile folios will be allowed on taxation.

The attorney will, I hope, always remain with us, for we have many honourable uses for him, and we shall continue to go to him for counsel when we are sick at heart, just as we go to our doctor when we are sick in body. The modern doctor has long ago given up the bloodletting business and has abandoned the forceful methods of the blue pill and the black draught, and nowadays he makes fame and fortune by endeavouring to conciliate your method of living with the capacity of your liver. It must not be thought that the proposal of Conciliation Courts is put forward with any desire to wreck and destroy the great profession of the law. On the contrary, men like Lord Brougham and Abraham Lincoln, who consistently preached the duty of the lawyer to promote peace among his neighbours, were the very men to stalwartly defend the lawyers' rights and privileges. Both were leaders in the front rank of the practice of advocacy and upheld the great traditions of a profession they practised with honour to themselves and their calling. Indeed, it has always been those who loved their profession best who have sought to rescue it from the ill name that has been cast upon it through the greed and selfishness of a small minority and the undue conservatism of the majority.

We may look forward without dismay to an age that will find far more useful and honourable duties for the attorney of the future, and there is no reason why these new duties should be less remunerative. No civilised country can exist without a pure system of the administration of justice, and that will always need a trained professional class inspired by noble traditions. And, though I may not myself witness the introduction of Conciliation Courts, I have not the least doubt that the common sense of the citizens of the country will insist upon their adoption, and the wisdom of lawyers will in the end welcome their institution among us. I do not see in the near future a land without lawyers, but in the new world I seriously believe that, in private as in public affairs, we shall strive more earnestly after peace, and the Law Society of the future will adopt as their official motto, "Blessed are the Peacemakers."

Chapter IV: *Concerning Daniel O'Connell*

TO the world at large Daniel O'Connell was known as "The Liberator," but to his friends and neighbours he was "The Counsellor." There is an atmosphere of intimacy and affectionate regard about the old word "counsellor" that cannot be said to surround the modern abbreviation "counsel." "Counsellor" suggests advice, "counsel" connotes fees. Counsellor Pleydell could never have been the same shrewd, loyal, jovial, lovable character under the designation Pleydell, K.C. There is an aroma in the word "Counsellor" that recalls going circuit in a post-chaise and sleeping at strange inns, and sitting round the circuit table watching the members drop one by one on to the floor. In Ireland it was to "The Counsellor" that the peasant went in his trouble, for it was he alone who could stand up to the Crown prosecutor, and bandy words with the judge, and bully the perjured witnesses of the prosecution into truth or shame.

Daniel O'Connell, in his career at the Bar, was rightly acclaimed by the people as "The Counsellor." He remained a stuff-gownsman to the end; he never asked for silk, and refused the judgeship offered to him. No Government ennobled him. He had two titles, but they were given him by his fellow-men. In the greater world of politics he was " The Liberator " ; in his own demesne in Kerry, on the Munster Circuit and among the peasantry of the West he was " The Counsellor."

By birth and nature Daniel O'Connell was Irish of the Irish. He was born on August 6, 1775, a mile up the creek from the little town of Cahirciveen, in the barony of Iveragh, in the south-west of Kerry, a country he loved to the last. Macdonagh tells us that he came of an ancient Gaelic sept, and that for a hundred years back his ancestors were farmers at Darrynane. Like all good Irish, Scots, and Welsh, he was proud of his ancestry, and did not easily bear to be crossed in his estimation of their worth. His enemies loved to taunt him with the fact that he was a grandson of a village tradesman, and had no right to the prefix O' to his name Connell.

" The vagabond lies ! " he exclaimed on reading a sketch of his life in which this was stated. " My father's family were very ancient, and my mother was a lady of the first rank." When, however, in later years, he was appealing to large audiences of the English democracy, he would boast : " I have no pride of ancestry. I am the son of a grazier or gentleman farmer."

In the first four years of his life O'Connell was brought up in an Irish cabin, and learned the Irish tongue from the foster-brothers and sisters with whom he played on the mud floor. He never knew a word of English until he was four years old. From this date until he first left home in 1790 for a school at Cork he ran wild in West Kerry. Had nature intended him for a Counsellor he could have had no better early education for the profession before him. As Macdonagh writes, " He joined in all the dances and hurling matches of the peasantry; he learned their songs and absorbed their favourite airs as they were played on bagpipes and fiddle at the festive gatherings. He heard their stories told in the Gaelic tongue by the blazing turf fires in the cabins during the long winter evenings—the hero tales, the folk-lore, the wild and beautiful legends, the superstitions, and the stories of the saints and holy places of Iveragh." This was his preparatory schooling. It may, as Mr. Pickwick imagined in a similar case, have been "rather a dangerous process," but it cannot be doubted that it gave O'Connell that deep insight to Irish character that few leaders of men have ever attained.

We may pass over his education in a Catholic college at Douay and his "eating a certain number of legs of mutton in London," which he did in the Hall of Lincoln's Inn, thereby becoming qualified to practise the law. He was called to the Bar May 19, 1798, and soon jumped into fame. In his third year he made over four hundred pounds, and when he was thirty-two years old his income was over two thousand, five hundred. From this figure it rose to eight thousand a year, a gigantic income for a junior barrister at the Irish Bar.

But in his early days he was by no means well off, and one of the elders of the Bar is said to have given him some good advice in the first year of his call. "If, my young friend, you will follow what I am going to tell you, I shall show you how to save fifty pounds a year for seven years."

O'Connell listened eagerly.

"Don't go circuit," said the old gentleman, with a chuckle.

But the lure of circuit was bound to appeal to a nature like Daniel O'Connell's. The adventure of it, the travelling, the fellowship, the change and excitement, the hope of fame—these were things he loved, and the zest of them remained with him to the end of his days. He was out for big game and ready to take risks, and in a very few years he found the gains on circuit exceeded the expenses. He joined the Munster Circuit, which included Clare, Limerick, Cork, and his own beloved Kerry. In after years he used to speak almost with regret about the improvement in roads and methods of communication. Twenty to thirty miles was a good day's journey in his early days, and at the end of each stage was an excellent inn.

Of these the inn at Millstreet must indeed have been a model if O'Connell's memory is to be trusted. " I well remember," he said, " when it was the regular end of the first day's journey from Tralee. It was a comfortable thing for a social pair of fellow-travellers to get out of their chaise at nightfall, and to find at the inn, then kept by a cousin of mine—a Mrs. Cotter—a roaring fire in a clean, well-furnished parlour, the whitest table linen, the best beef, the sweetest and tenderest mutton, the fattest fowl, the most excellent wine (claret and madeira were the high wines then—they knew nothing about champagne), and the most comfortable beds."

O'Connells circuit triumphs spread to Dublin, and it was not long before he saw his picture in a magazine in a shop window, and laughed as he reminded himself that his " boyish dreams of glory " were attained. There was no more popular figure in all the Munster assize towns and folk would gaze lovingly after their handsome countryman and point him out with pride to the stranger, " That's Counsellor O'Connell, God bless him."

In reading some of his feats of advocacy, one is a little uncertain at times as to whether he is quite " playing the game," but we must remember that the Irish game is and always has been played under different rules from ours. The members of the Bench were not always competent, courteous, or fair in their dealings. They belonged to a different clan from the prisoner, who in many cases neither expected nor obtained justice. The Crown and the Crown witnesses were huntsmen and dogs, out to run the man in the dock to the death. Prisoner's counsel had no right to address the jury, and therefore it was only by putting irrelevant questions and arguing their validity that any form of speech could be made. O'Connell was an adept at making a series of interjectional speeches to a jury during the progress of the case, and no judge or Crown prosecutor could prevent him. He would ask a Crown witness some wholly improper questions, which always had the effect of bringing the Crown prosecutor on to his legs, with: " My Lord, I object to that question."

One can see the pleasant smile on O'Connell's broad features, and the genial twinkle in his blue eyes, as he begins a long argument to the judge for the benefit of the jury.

" My Lord, I had every right to put the question. It is quite material, and I am surprised at my friend's objections. If the witness answers in the affirmative, it is plain as a pikestaff my client is entitled to an acquittal, and if in the negative it contradicts the case stated by the Crown," etc.

To understand O'Connell's great merits as an advocate, one must always remember the kind of Courts in which he worked.

The legend of his first brief is well authenticated, and the story is a classic on the Munster Circuit. It was at Limerick Assizes, and the case was one of aggravated assault, in which he appeared for the defence. His opportunity came in cross-examination of the prosecutor.

If you can get the Irish rhythm and accent into the words, you can see the scene before you, the baffled witness on the table, the merry bantering counsel at the Bar, and the ragged crowd keenly watching the contest.

" On your oath now," began O'Connell, " how much drink had you taken before the fight began ? "

" Troth, not very much."

" Did you not have a pint of potheen a man ? "

" Well, I had my share of a pint."

" What quantity did you drink ? How much was your share ? "

" 'Twas a good sup."

" On your solemn oath now," said O'Connell, nailing him, " did not your share of the pint of potheen consist of it all except the pewter ? "

" Well then, dear knows, but that's true for you, sir."

And the laughter that greeted the admission was the measure of the Counsellor's first success.

Many stories are told of O'Connell's capacity for ruling the Bench either by intellect, cajolery, or sheer force of character. On one occasion he was defending two men for robbery, and called a young priest to give evidence to character. Judge Torrens, who tried the case, seemed to think that the precise and somewhat affected language of the priest amounted to equivocation, and rudely told him to stand down.

Up jumped O'Connell as the young priest shuffled off the table, and in tones of deep commiseration turned to the dock and cried: "Ah, my poor fellows, bigotry is on the bench, and when your excellent young priest has been so ignominiously turned out of Court I am in despair of being able to serve you. Here's your brief and fee." He flung the brief and the notes to the agent for the prisoners and commenced putting on his cloak, muttering: "My innocent clients, I despair altogether now of your acquittal; you'll be hanged, and never were men hanged more unjustly. The only hope I can look to is that if your sentence is not carried into execution before the twelve judges meet I bring this outrageous case before them."

This so terrified Judge Torrens that he begged O'Connell to continue the defence, which after much protest he did, and the Judge, in summing up, made much more of the priest's evidence of honesty than it really amounted to. The men were acquitted.

Judge Day was a judicial weakling, and fair sport for the advocates. Curran said of him that to see him grapple with a point of law was like watching a man open an oyster with a rolling-pin. The Judge knew his own deficiencies, and once at Cork Assizes said to O'Connell: "Mr. O'Connell, I must not allow you to make a speech;

the fact is that I am always of opinion with the last speaker, and therefore I will not let you say one word."

"My Lord," replied O'Connell sternly, "that is precisely the reason why I'll let nobody have the last word but myself, if I can help it." This he did, with the result that the Judge had foreseen.

Judge Day must have been a standing temptation to the most scrupulous advocate. He would swallow any legal nonsense forcibly presented to him. It was a recognised part of the game, apparently, when defending a prisoner, to take any bogus point of law that came uppermost. It was like fly-fishing. If you could lure your judicial fish with a gawdy-coloured contraption that he was foolish enough to mistake for a real fly, you were considered an excellent sportsman. After all, the Judge was supposed to know the law, and if he did not it was acknowledged to be a fair thing to take advantage of his ignorance in the interest of the accused. O'Connell's most impudent success in this line was at the expense of Judge Day. The Counsellor's client was charged with stealing a goat. O'Connell produced an old Act of Parliament empowering the owners of cornfields, gardens, and plantations to kill and destroy goats. From this he argued that clearly goats were not property, and therefore not the subject of larceny. This argument appealed to Judge Day's mind so successfully that he charged the jury accordingly, and the prisoner was acquitted.

The Bench of Ireland at that date had not, for many reasons, the respect and affection of the people, and but for the independence and courage of the members of the Bar little justice would have been done. O'Connell was a man of the most fearless disposition, and not only insisted on judicial courtesy, and fair play to himself, but demanded it for his younger and less reliant juniors.

On a famous occasion a young barrister named John Martley was attempting to state a case to Lord Norbury and Judge Johnson. The former kept up a running commentary of puns, for which he was notorious, whilst Judge Johnson growled out interruptions at the unfortunate junior with ill-humour and impatience. The young barrister was floundering in confusion and O'Connell begged some of the leaders in court to interpose, but they would not. He could not witness this continued bullying without protest, and rising with calm dignity, he addressed the Bench.

" My Lords," he said, " I respectfully ask your lordships to hear this young gentleman. Mr. Martley is not personally known to me, but I submit he has a right to be heard."

" Oh, Mr. O'Connell, we have heard Mr. Martley," said Lord Norbury, " and we cannot allow the time of the Court to be further wasted."

" Pardon me, my Lord, you have not heard him. He has not been allowed to state his motion ; I am sure he is quite capable of doing so now if your lordships permit him."

" Mr. O'Connell," asked Judge Johnson, with an air of defiance, " are you engaged in this motion that you presume to interfere ? "

" My Lord, I am not," replied O'Connell ; " but I rise to defend the privileges of the Bar, and I will never permit them to be violated either in my own or the person of any other member of the profession."

O'Flanagan tells of a somewhat similar case, where a young counsel named Richards, who appeared for other parties in a Chancery case in which O'Connell held a brief, wanting to address the Court, the Lord Chancellor put him down, saying he had heard arguments on that point and had made up his mind. The counsel pressed to be heard. The Chancellor got angry and declared that he would not hear him.

" Well, then, my Lord," said O'Connell in his deepest and most emphatic tone, " since your lordship refuses to hear my learned friend, you will be pleased to hear ME," and plunging at once into the intricacies of the case, without waiting any expression of assent or dissent from the Chancellor, on went O'Connell, discussing and distinguishing the cases already cited, quoting others that were quite in point for his client, until he secured the attention and evidently made a very great impression upon the mind of the Lord Chancellor. Every five minutes, as he replied ably to some opponent or opened fresh ground, O'Connell would say, " Now, my Lord, my learned young friend beside me, had your lordship heard him, would have informed your lordship in a more impressive and lucid manner than I can hope to——"

It is no wonder, then, that the Counsellor was as popular with his fellow-barristers as he was with the public, and that his name at the Irish Bar will always be associated with ideals of manliness, independence, and courage.

The power of cross-examination was at this time the

only weapon that the advocate of the man in the dock could use. Speech was denied to him, and it was only by breaking down the Crown witnesses and disgracing them dramatically before the jury that an acquittal could be hoped for. All sorts of snares were laid for the untruthful, and O'Connell was an expert at the preparation of trouble for the perjurer.

At a trial at Ennis of two men for burning a police barracks, one of the main points of the prosecution was to prove that the fire was started by pitch. The chief witness for the prosecution swore that he discovered the barrack on fire, and knew it was set on fire by pitch, for he got the smell of it.

He was then cross-examined by O'Connell. "You know the smell of pitch, then?"

"I do well."

"You seem a man able to smell pitch anywhere?"

"Anywhere I found it."

"Even here in this Court-house if it was here."

"No doubt I would."

"And do you swear that you don't get the smell of pitch here?"

"I do solemnly; if it was here I'd smell it."

Then O'Connell, taking his broad-rimmed hat off the skillet of pitch which he had caused to be placed near the witness's chair said with a smile of triumph:

"Now you may go down, you perjured rascal; go down!"

This saved his client. The jury discredited the witness, and acquitted the prisoners.

In a case at Cork, O'Connell was successful with a bold,

if somewhat hazardous, ruse. The prisoner, whose name was James, was indicted for murder, and the chief Crown witness swore to finding the prisoner's hat near the scene of the murder. He was very emphatic that the hat belonged to James.

"Now," said O'Connell to the witness on cross-examination, "you are quite sure about this hat?"

"I am," replied the witness.

"Let me look at it again," said O'Connell, taking it from the witness and examining it carefully. He then looked inside, and spelled J-A-M-E-S. "Now do you mean to tell the Court and jury this name was in the hat when you found it?"

"I do, on my oath," replied the witness.

"Did you see the name, then?"

"I did—surely."

"This is the same hat, no mistake about it?"

"Och, no mistake—'tis his hat."

"And all you have sworn is as true as that?"

"Quite."

"Now you may go down," said O'Connell sternly. "My Lord, there is an end of this case—there is no name whatever in the hat." The result was a prompt acquittal.

Of the Counsellor's intuition and quickness of perception in guessing the secret in a lying witness's heart many stories are told. He certainly had a very intimate knowledge of the thoughts and feelings of the lower classes, but in the following story it is difficult to believe that he had not received some inkling of the real truth before he went to court. The story is told, however, as an example of his marvellous power of insight, and is in any case a curious record of humour, villainy, and superstition.

It was a will case, and the validity of the will was in dispute. The witnesses for the defence all swore that the testator had signed the will while "life was in him." Other counsel had cross-examined the witnesses, and the last witness was handed over to O'Connell. He, too, swore by the same phrase that "life was in the testator when the will was signed."

"By virtue of your oath was he alive?" asked O'Connell.

"By virtue of my oath life was in him."

"Now," continued O'Connell, with great solemnity and assuming an air of inspiration, "I call on you, in the presence of your Maker, before Whom you must one day be judged for the evidence you give here to-day, I solemnly ask—and answer me at your peril—was it not a live fly that was in the dead man's mouth when his hand was placed on the will?"

The witness fell on his knees, and confessed that they had indeed placed a fly in the mouth of the deceased, that they might swear "that life was in him."

One of O'Connell's last and greatest triumphs was the defence of the Doneraile conspirators. A murder had taken place, and the authorities proceeded to round up all and sundry into the dock, and a special commission was sent down to try them at Cork. The first batch of five prisoners was found guilty on most unsatisfactory evidence, and sentenced to be hanged in six days. One of these was a respectable old farmer of nearly seventy, who rented a farm of over £200 a year. He was firmly believed to be innocent, and these convictions struck terror and dismay through the countryside. There was but one thought in every mind : O'Connell must be sent for. He was then at Kerry, ninety miles away. The convictions took place on Saturday afternoon, and another lot of prisoners was to be tried on Monday morning at nine o'clock.

William Burke, of Bally-hea, was the messenger, and on Sunday morning he was at Darrynane in the Counsellor's presence. " I left Cork yesterday evening at five o'clock and rode all night, ninety long miles, to see your honour. The friends of the poor boys that are in the dock for the Doneraile conspiracy sent me to you, and unless you are in Cork before the Court opens every man of them will be hanged, though as innocent as the child unborn."

O'Connell was fifty-six years old at this time, but he was vigorous and strong, and a fast gig took him over the mountains in the black of night. Burke had gone ahead, and great was the excitement when it was heard that the Counsellor was on his way. The Judges were asked to postpone the hearing, but refused, Baron Pennefather declaring " the trials should proceed without delay."

Scouts were placed along the Killarney road, but no news came. The jury were sworn, and the Solicitor-General had risen to address the jury when a loud, increasing volume of cheers arose and swept towards the Court-house. It was not possible to hear anything but the shouts of popular joy. " The Counsellor is come ! "

How he took his seat at the Bar in his travelling robes ; how he munched sandwiches and supped a bowl of milk whilst he corrected the Solicitor-General's law between each mouthful ; how he bantered and bullied the Crown witnesses, and how Nowlan, the most infamous of them, broke down in his lies and howled in agony : " Wisha then God knows 'tis little I thought I'd meet you here to-day, Counsellor O'Connell. May the Lord save me from you ! "—these things are all faithfully recorded in the chronicles of the trial.

The jury, though kept without food for a day and a half, disagreed, a further batch of prisoners was acquitted, and then the Crown abandoned the prosecutions and reprieved those already convicted. Small wonder the Counsellor was beloved throughout the land.

O'Connell himself had many quaint stories of the curious manner in which his poorer clients would try to express their gratitude to him. He was fond of telling a typical Irish incident of a sturdy fellow from the hills, who, being acquitted at Cork, thanked him with tears in his eyes, saying : " Och, Counsellor ! I've no way *here* to show your honour my gratitude, but I wisht I saw you knocked down in my own parish, and maybe I wouldn't bring a faction to your rescue."

Another of his clients, who was acquitted upon a technical point of stealing a cow at night, was asked by O'Connell how he managed to steal the fattest cow in the dark. He was delighted to be able to tell the Counsellor something he did not know. " Why, then, I'll tell your honour the whole secret of that, sir. Whenever your honour goes to steal a cow, always go on the worst night you can, for if the weather is very bad the chances are that nobody will be up to see your honour. The way you'll always know the fat cattle in the dark is by this token—that the fat cows always stand in the most exposed places, but the lean ones always go into the ditch for shelter."

One point in O'Connell's methods of advocacy that was very notable was his power of vituperation, in which, though he had many rivals, he appears to have been unsurpassed by any member of the Irish Bar. He had a tolerably good tongue for inventing at the moment epithets of abuse that seemed to his hearers to fit the occasion. He was fighting a case against an attorney who constantly interrupted him with futile and absurd objections, urged with considerable rudeness and pertinacity. O'Connell stood the annoyance for some time with more or less patience, and at length fastened him with a stern look and shouted at him in tones that reverberated through the Court-house: "Sit down, you snarling, pugnacious Ram Cat!"

The attorney was quelled, the court rocked with laughter, and the sobriquet remained with the unfortunate man for ever. It must have been incidents like this that caused the old crier in Ennis to try and clear the court by shouting out: "All ye blackguards that isn't lawyers quit the court," a phrase that delighted O'Connell beyond measure.

But if there was a touch of genial ruffianism in O'Connell's advocacy, no doubt it was necessary in the day in which he lived, for it was a day of sledge-hammers rather than pin-pricks. O'Connell was no greater a sinner than any other advocate, but his abuse was more original and epigrammatic than most. The picture of his home life that we have from many sources shows that at heart he was of a just, kindly, generous nature. In a happier generation there is no doubt that O'Connell would have made an ideal Irish Judge. At his home at Darrynane, where he was much beloved, he would find on his return from the hunt a large number of peasants from the surrounding county waiting for him to arbitrate in their disputes. These he heard and determined at his gate, the proceedings being held in the Irish tongue, and his decisions were never disputed, nor was there ever an effort made to re-try a case before a more regular tribunal.

It is true that in 1838 the offer was made to him of the office of Lord Chief Baron, but he declined it, although it went to his heart to refuse a position which would leave him free in April to join his beloved beagles " just when the jack hares leave the most splendid trails in the mountains." But nothing could keep O'Connell from what he considered his mission in life. The joys of his home, the pleasures of sport, the glory of a great forensic career, were all gladly sacrificed to what he deemed to be the call of his country. Eighteen years before his death, at the height of his fame, he relinquished his practice at the Bar. To use his own words :

" I flung away my profession, I gave its emoluments to the winds, I closed the vista of its honours and dignities, I embraced the cause of my country, and, come weal or come woe, I have made a choice at which I have never repined, nor shall ever repent."

Chapter V : *Concerning the Passing of the Indictment*

> "Here is th' indictment of the good Lord Hastings;
> Which in a set hand fairly is engross'd,
> That it may be to-day read o'er in Paul's:
> And mark how well the sequel hangs together:—
> Eleven hours I have spent to write it over."
>
> *Richard III*, Act III, Scene vi.

THROUGH the long ages of our history, the Indictment, that dread instrument of the Law, has continued through its outward shape and inward legal form to symbolise in its parchment permanence and quaint mysterious phrasing the ancientry of our legal institutions. How many sheep and lambs have gone to the slaughter—their wool taken for sacks for Chancellors to sit on, perchance, their mutton comfortably digested by the unthinking mob—that their skins might be preserved for the engrossment of horrid crimes, and that the wicked ones in the dock, comforted with the solemn parchment record of their sins, might tremble before the Clerk of Assize as he mumbled out the mysterious arraignment from the counts of the never-ending parchment roll that doomed the evil doer to the gallows. That the Law should be no respecter of persons is well, but that it should treat our most ancient historical institutions without due reverence is hardly to be borne.

> "Let wealth and commerce, laws and learning die,
> But leave us still our old nobility."

Concerning the Passing of the Indictment

And what has more nobility in form, language, and historical tradition than the Indictment of our Common Law? If such an institution is to be abolished without protest, our oldest nobility may well be in danger of judgment. Yet here, without a word of explanation or consolation, comes along a King's Printer's copy of a little thin, flippant statute calling itself "Indictments Act, 1915, alias 5 & 6 Geo. V. Ch. 90," and we find to our dismay that the Indictment—that entertaining miscellany of our criminal courts, at once the Palladium of our liberties and the Coliseum of our Constitution—has passed away, unwept, unhonoured, and unsung.

I remember long ago on a Sunday afternoon a little child in a nursery, whose sole Sabbath reading was "Line upon Line," an undramatic version of the Old Testament, was discovered by her elders sitting on the hearth-rug weeping as if her heart would break. For a long time she refused to tell her grief, but at length, in answer to the tender questions of her parents, she sobbed out the mournful news: "Oh, Mummy, Aaron's dead!"

It can scarcely be that the career of Aaron had captivated her young idea, but she had spelled through long pages of his respectable history. There seemed every reason to hope he had lived down the memory of that little incident about the golden calf, and now, just as she fondly imagined he had settled down to a permanent ecclesiastical sinecure, the news came that they had carried him to the top of a mountain, taken away his garments, and left him alone to die.

When I read "Indictments Act, 1915," I seemed to remember that little child and fully entered into her feelings. I felt tears in my own throat to think that my ancient friend the Indictment, once generous to me even in guineas, was no more. I, too, longed to sit on a hearth-rug and sob until some Alma Mater would come to console me in my sorrow.

One hesitates to reveal to sober citizens the true frightfulness of the details of this iconoclastic statute. It is even enacted that parchment is no longer necessary, "durable paper" may be used. One knows what that means. Imagine indicting Sir Walter Raleigh for treason on wood pulp! Again, the Indictment need not be joined together in one roll. In the old days it was some small satisfaction and pride to the poor fellow in the dock to see his false pretences set out with due averment and scientific negation on long rolls of sheepskin; now he will have to listen to a bald catalogue of his crimes from sheets of paper twelve inches square bound in book form. True, it is enacted that "a proper margin not less than three inches in width shall be kept on the left-hand side of each sheet"—a touch of the vanished hand of your old scrivener here—but alas! if this good order is disobeyed it does not appear that the unfortunate man in the dock has any remedy. He cannot plead in abatement, or bring a writ of error, or move to quash, or perform any of those ancient legal gymnastics that used to bring him relief.

When one comes to the form of the futurist Indictment it is even more heartrending. It is like gazing at a beautiful ancient city whose noblest and most ancient towers and landmarks have been brutally destroyed. No longer do you describe to the unhappy wretch in the dock exactly what he has done in mysterious language and terms of art and words he does not understand, thereby buoying him up with a hope that you may have made a mess of it altogether, and by that means he may slip out of your net. Nowadays you simply tell him that he murdered so and so on such a day and go on with the case. The absence of dignity about such a crude and coarse proceeding in itself condemns it.

All the old rules are gone. Felonies and misdemeanours may be huddled together in the same Indictment—a monstrous indecency. We shall hear next of anarchists desiring to abolish the time-honoured distinction between felonies and misdemeanours, an outrage happily almost impossible, since no one really knows why any particular crime should be one rather than the other. Popularly it may be said that the scientific difference between them is akin to the subtle diversity of attorneys and solicitors or alligators and crocodiles.

Those consolatory religious averments with which the pious draftsmen brought to the mind of the criminal the origin of all sin and crime will never again adorn the Indictment. Surely some Bishop in the House of Lords might have stood out for the maintenance of the established form " not having the fear of God before his eyes, but being moved and seduced by the instigation of the devil." I remember a Sheriff's chaplain who always closed his eyes when the Clerk of Assize read out these words. They were legally useless, perhaps, but quite harmless, for they had always been regarded as averments not necessary to be proved, the Court taking judicial notice of the instigation of the Evil One, but sternly refusing to regard it as any sort of excuse for the crime, and never permitting it to be mentioned in mitigation of punishment.

How careful they were in the old days. One count of the Indictment would allege that the murderer was holding his knife in the right hand, another count thought it was his left, another alleged neither hand, and the last count always wound up by saying the victim was murdered by means to the said jury unknown. Mr. Justice Stephen seemed to think that the fact that the Clerks of Assize were paid by fees, which were calculated at so much a count, had something to do with these artful distinctions ; but for my part I scout the suggestion and believe it was due to industry and a love of art for art's sake.

No more shall we see rolling ample indictments covering many yards of honest parchment, full of goodly sounding idioms, blossoming into a hundred counts, confounding the prisoner and the Evil One and all their wicked ways. All, all are gone, the old familiar phrases ; and indeed there is a special section in the statute warning us that if we use them in the good old way we do it at our own risk as to costs.

I think my respect and affection for the Indictment dates back to my early days on the Northern Circuit, when I sat at the feet of two old champions of the Sessions and heard their tales of still more ancient times when pleas in abatement, demurrers, and sur-rebutters were part of legal human nature's daily food. Alas ! good Cottingham and Foard, what would a world without Indictments have been to you ?

"Old Cot.," as he was lovingly called, had a mind steeped in the criminal legal lore of old days. Irish to the backbone, and at Bar Mess a courteous, kindly gentleman, in court, with his back to the dock, he was a fierce and acrid fighter. Foard had small knowledge of the criminal law but a large store of miscellaneous reading, and was really learned in Shaksperean matter, but his scholarship was marred by a treacherous memory. Charles Russell once described him as a "mine of inaccurate information," which had just the taste of truth about it to make the fun not unkindly.

Between Cottingham and Foard there was no love lost. They were always defending or prosecuting against each other, and the pedantic lawyer regarded the fantastic scholar with unconcealed contempt. Cottingham would tell you the best stories of Foard, and Foard knew the choicest anecdotes about Cottingham. The latter revelled in descriptions of Foard's jury eloquence. Foard had long Dundreary whiskers, a wide mouth, and a very solemn, learned face, and was not wholly unlike the late Mr. Justice Day. He never tired of Shaksperean quotations, and, according to Cottingham, never quoted them accurately.

On one occasion he was defending a herbalist for selling some poisonous drugs, and his mind slowly worked round to "Romeo and Juliet" and the passage commencing:

> "I do remember an apothecary
> And hereabouts he dwells——"

towards the introduction of which he clumsily steered his oration. At length he got near to his harbour, when his unfortunate memory deserted him, and he laboured to a conclusion, as follows :—

" Gentlemen, my unfortunate client was very much in the position of the apothecary in that beautiful play 'Romeo and Juliet.' Shakspere, you will remember, gentlemen—Shakspere, I repeat, a name of which every Englishman must be proud—The Bard, as he is universally called, in that play, or shall we call it a poem, in words that might have been used to portray my client's situation—Shakspere! Hm! The Bard! Hm! The Swan of Avon—I forget, gentlemen, the actual words he used, but the purport of the passage is that there was a chemist and druggist living round the corner."

To see Cottingham taking a plea in abatement was indeed a solemn sight. When he " moved to quash," he pronounced the word of art to rhyme with " bash " and not " bosh," and he smacked his lips over it in a savage and hungry manner.

He was rarely successful, but once I remember Foard had drafted a large number of counts charging a man with several offences under a statute, and Cottingham came into his kingdom. There were occasional Shaksperean phrases in the Indictment, which was of a chatty nature, but the words of the statute in that case made and provided were but vaguely referred to or wholly absent.

Cottingham rose like a tiger and moved or almost sprang to quash. Count by count he argued, showing that no offence known to the Law had been set out, and count by count the logical mind of Mr. Justice Henn Collins was forced to agree with him. In the end Foard arose, and after remembering with great effect the lines from "Richard III," "Eleven hours I have spent to write it over," solemnly read it word by word with evident literary affection to the weary Judge.

"But, really, Mr. Foard, can you point me out a single count which charges any offence under the statute?" asked the Judge, in despair.

"Possibly not," replied the learned counsel, "but what does your lordship think of the legal effect of all the counts taken together?"

"The literary effect is excellent, Mr. Foard," said the Judge, with his sweetest smile, "but I fear that the legal effect is nothing."

Cottingham was by no means always successful, indeed it was otherwise, for he would raise and argue any defence, however wild, or start any point against an Indictment, however hopeless. He was the Don Quixote of the dock. At the County Sessions he was defending a lad for stealing a neighbour's canary. It was a dead case, and Foard was full of joy at the prospective hope of downing his opponent, when Cottingham, with an air of victory, jumped up and moved to quash the Indictment. Foard was dismayed, the more so as Higgin, K.C., the Chairman, who delighted in Cottingham's objections, pretended to take the deepest interest in this one.

"I apprehend, sir," said Cottingham, as Higgin nodded approval, "that this Indictment will not lie. It is well known that there cannot be any property in what are called *ferae naturae*, that is to say, wild animals, whether they be beasts or birds, and it appears on the Indictment that this bird is a canary, and as all canaries are in their very nature wild birds of an alien country, they are therefore *ferae naturae*, and not the subject of larceny."

Higgin solemnly called upon Foard to answer this plea, and after Foard had finished, without throwing any great light on the matter, Higgin took up the Indictment and said, " I see, Mr. Cottingham, the Indictment charges that your client stole ' a certain canary and cage.' What about the cage ? "

" The cage ? " repeated Cottingham, by no means taken aback. " The cage ? Why, that, sir, is no difficulty; the cage is, of course, merely ancillary to the bird."

The picture of a canary flying about with an ancillary cage attached to it was too much for Higgin, who laughingly suggested that Mr. Cottingham had better take the jury's opinion on his client's innocence.

Mischievous juniors were apt to amuse themselves with Cottingham's love and fear of Indictments. He was once prosecuting in a perjury case, and had drafted a very lengthy Indictment for perjury and subornation that made a huge, handsome parchment scroll of accusation on the Clerk of Assize's desk.

The defending junior made great play of studying it line by line in the library and consulting his brethren about it, and then in a kindly way informed Cottingham that the engrosser had made a horrible blunder in it that would make it necessary for him to move to quash. Cottingham then went through it in detail, but could find nothing wrong, and he asked his learned friends their views, who all agreed that the point was probably fatal, but would not tell him what it was.

The night before the trial the humble junior allowed the point to be wormed out of him at Bar Mess. In the phrase " took his corporal oath on the Gospel of God," he explained that the engrosser had spelt Gospel and God with two small " g's," thereby making the Indictment bad for blasphemy. Everyone round the table who was in the conspiracy agreed with this view. Cottingham contended weakly against it as he was the only one of the company who thought anything of it, and his fears, as he admitted openly, were greatly strengthened by the fact that the prisoner was to be tried by the late Lord Chief Justice Coleridge, whose holiness was proverbial.

The point was, of course, never taken, but to one of Cottingham's years and training it was not wholly ridiculous. He could remember the procedure of an age when, if a man was indicted as Richard James Smith and turned out to be James Richard Smith, or if his surname was wrongly spelled and the error of spelling sounded different from the correct name, the doctrine of *idem sonans* was solemnly discussed and in all probability the Indictment was quashed and the prisoner set free.

Indeed, in the early days it is almost wonderful that anyone was ever convicted, and there are volumes of reports containing the considered judgments of the most learned judges setting aside Indictments on what we now consider to be absurd and frivolous pretexts. The life of " The Monster," as he was called, a man named Renwick Williams, whose picture you may find in the " Newgate Calendar " stabbing Miss Anne Porter in the streets, was saved by the draftsman of the Indictment. He was charged with assaulting her with intent to cut her clothes, and the Indictment said that he assaulted her and did cut her clothes ; but this way of doing it charged him with two offences, assault and cutting clothes, which, as the Judges said, might have happened on different days. It should have said assaulted and *did then and there* cut her clothes. So for the want of those few words Renwick Williams escaped the gallows. No wonder Mr. Justice Stephen should say that " the law relating to Indictments was much as if some small portion of the prisoners convicted had been allowed to toss up for their liberty."

But on occasion the old Judges would stand out for common sense and public policy—charm the pleaders never so wisely with their technicalities. The case of Sir Charles Sedley is in point. You will find the story of it in " Pepys' Diary " and Johnson's " Lives of the Poets," and the law of it in the black-letter of old Siderfin.

Sir Charles, with his friends Lord Buckhurst and Sir Thomas Ogle, got very drunk at the Cock Tavern in Bow Street, a disreputable place kept by one " Oxford Kate," after which, Pepys tells us, he came out on to the balcony naked and preached a lewd mountebank sermon to the mob, and wound up by drinking the King's health. In the legal jargon of that day the charge was that he did " monstre son nude Corps in un Balcony in Covent Garden al grand multitude de people," and the question for the Court was whether this beastly form of drunken revelry was a misdemeanour " encounter le Peace del Roy." The added humour of the situation lay in the fact that the Roy himself was, as like as not, one of the party and art and part in the escapade, for Charles II affected the society of Sedley and his friends, and on occasion honoured them by getting drunk in their company.

It was strenuously argued that the gallant baronet was entitled at common law to appear in public with nothing on if he so desired, and that to indict him for misdemeanour for so doing was an attack upon the liberty of the subject, no such offence being known to the Law. An endeavour was made to portray the defendant as a champion of the principles of freedom and voluntaryism as against the powers of restraint and compulsion. This, with the known friendship of the Court and the absence of precedent for the Indictment, was expected to pull him through.

But here, in the words of Serjeant Arabin, " the hand of Justice steps in and says," and its say from the lips of that upright Lord Chief Justice, Sir Robert Foster, was very straight and to the point.

The Court swept aside all sophistries about precedents and Indictments. This conduct they declared to be against good manners and therefore a misdemeanour at common law, and, as Pepys tells us, " my Lord and the rest of the Judges did all of them round give Sir Charles Sedley a most high reproof ; my Lord Chief Justice saying that it was for him and such wicked wretches as he was that God's anger and judgments hung over us, calling him sirrah many times." At the same time they tempered the wind to the shorn lamb, and on the ground that he was a gentleman of ancient family in the county of Kent, with an encumbered estate, fined him two thousand marks or in the alternative seven days.

This decision was really a very brave and honourable

affair. A few years afterwards Sedley got into another drunken scrape and was arrested by the watch, whereupon Lord Chief Justice Keeling laid the constable by the heels, which, as Pepys said, was a " horrid shame " ; but this was far more in keeping with the judicial practice of the age than the honest conduct of Lord Chief Justice Foster and his colleagues.

It is encouraging and refreshing to read of cases where judicial common sense and right thinking overcome the defects in the machinery of the law. At the end of the eighteenth century a discussion arose on an Indictment as to whether it was an offence known to the law to take up a dead body for the purposes of dissection. There were Jacobean statutes against stealing dead bodies for the purposes of witchcraft, but that was another matter. Serjeant Bond, for the defence, was very plausible. He admitted fairly enough that digging up the body was a trespass to the soil, and maybe taking away the shroud was an injury to the executors, but how could it be an indictable offence to remove a body which belonged to nobody?

The great Garrow, who prosecuted, was very half-hearted about it. A long experience of Indictments at the Old Bailey probably made him suspicious of their face value, and he merely mildly suggested that as the body was taken for the purposes of dissection that probably made a difference.

It was one of those cases where modern Judges often fold their hands and regretfully complain that they have no power to remedy the wrong done. But this happened in the time of Lord Chief Justice Kenyon, when the spacious traditions of Lord Mansfield were fresh in men's minds. The Court made small work of all this humming and hawing about technicalities. Common decency required that such an offence should be put a stop to—they appealed again to the code of good manners which should govern men's actions, their nature revolted at such practices, and they refused to allow it to be discussed, "lest that alone should convey to the public an idea that they entertained a doubt respecting the crime alleged."

In such style, on right occasion, did the Judges of old burst through the straits of law into the open sea of justice. They understood that it was a law of Nature that freedom should slowly broaden down from precedent to precedent, and they supplied the necessary precedents. Their instinct discerned that law must stand four-square with decency, morality, and the good of the people, whatever the letter of it spelt, or else it must fail in its purpose. When one reads these bold decisions, one must admire their downright English simplicity of thought and purpose, and recognise that it has always been that capacity for honest thinking and right action that has kept the Judges of our country respected in the land, in spite of the wild absurdity of much of the law they have to administer. This must have been the meaning of Lord Russell of Killowen when he reminded an old circuit friend who was beginning his career as a Judge of the County Court, "that it was better to be strong and wrong than weak and right." The idea is perhaps expressed with more finesse in the already famous paradox of Lord Reading, when he told the American Bar, "The idea that it is the duty of the Law Courts to dispense law is becoming obsolete. It is recognised that the true duty of the Courts is to dispense justice."

But while we turn over the worn yellow pages of the old law reports and smile at the solemn pribbles and prabbles of Indictment points, do not let us forget that a hundred years hence many of our legal decisions will appear just as childish to our great-grandchildren as these are to us. I could match some of the narrowest Indictment decisions with specimens of reported cases under the Workmen's Compensation Act. For the true type of judicial mind will always prefer to chew the words of a statute rather than to breathe the spirit of it. We inherit that frame of mind, I suppose, from our priestly ancestors who, as Charles Lamb reminds us, loved to defend or oppugn such *Theses Quaedam Theologicae* as "Whether the Archangel Uriel could knowingly affirm an untruth, and whether if he *could* he *would*."

And for my part I confess to a love of the old days, and have a reverent affection for all these absurd traditional formalities. I do not like to see the legal furniture of our forefathers broken up and thrown on the scrap heap.

> "Wherever I turn my head
> There's a mildew and a mould;
> The sun's going out over-head
> And I'm very old."

And so I suppose it is the Old Adam in me that rebels against such trifling official pamphlets as "Indictments Act, 1915," and I look back on the age of Cottingham as a golden age, and even have dreams of regret for the far-gone past when Court-hand and Latin were the letters and language of our law. One dreads these legal reforms coming like a thief in the night and removing our ancient landmarks. One feels, to use a modern figure, that the great legal omnibus is side-slipping into Chaos.

For if Indictments are to be ruthlessly pruned in this way, where are we to stop? What is to prevent some high-brow legal reformer seizing a big blue pencil and striking out as embarrassing and irrelevant great chunks of the muddy verbosity that we call Rules of Court and throwing big lumps of the practice books to the rag merchant?

When I first read the Indictments Act fresh from the King's printer's press I shuddered at its iconoclasm, but as I read I smiled and took heart of grace. For when I reached Section 9 I found that "This Act shall come into operation on the first day of April." There was a hopeful consonance about that date. Were there jesters abroad in high places? Was I perchance dreaming, and were these official pages mere *simulacra* and no real statute at all? I was half convinced that when the clock struck twelve on the first day of April I should find the good old Indictment secure in its ancient supremacy and the mocking words "April Fool!" ringing in my long ears.

But alas! the thing was only too true. The hour struck, but the bell knolled for the passing of the Indictment. Let us hope that the news of it has not carried across the Styx and that the shades of Foard and Cottingham are untroubled by the shame of it.

Chapter VI: *Concerning the Psychology of Perjury*

"WHAT is truth?" asked jesting Pilate, and would not stay for an answer. Pilate is not the only stipendiary who has had the same question haunting his thoughts as he listens to so-called evidence. We seek to make every trial an inquest of truth, but owing to human naughtiness, faulty machinery, carelessness, and selfishness we have not as yet perfected in our courts the noble art of arriving at the truth, the whole truth, and nothing but the truth.

The English-speaking races have always worshipped truth and based their power on national veracity. Alfred the Great was known to the Normans as "the truth speaker." George Washington, who "did it with his little hatchet," *could not* tell a lie, though, as Mark Twain asserted with some show of reason, his was the superior moral attitude, since he *could* lie readily, but refrained from doing so.

Yet, in spite of our national truthful habit and a general desire in the community to give true evidence, those who visit our courts come away with an uneasy idea that there is a great deal of perjury committed at almost every trial. Yet if in a future age the history of our times is written by a professor who bases his work solely upon official statistics he will pronounce our generation to be scrupulously truthful and free from the crime of perjury. Look, he will say, at multitudinous legal proceedings taking place in Police Courts, County Courts, High Courts, and before arbitrators, consider the number of affidavits made in one year, and then turn to the Criminal Statistics of 1920, and you will find that only forty-five citizens were convicted of perjury. What a splendid record of veracity! How scrupulous and careful must these people have been in giving their testimony in the law courts! How greatly devoted was this pious generation to the pursuit of truth!

Nor would our professor be so hopelessly wrong in his verdict. The martyr of the witness-box often honestly intends to sacrifice himself on the altar of truth and finds to his dismay that he has made a pickle-herring farce of the business. Truth, after all, is a very vague and abstract affair, and the man in the street would find it hard to answer Pilate with an apt definition. On the other hand, most of us could define a lie. The schoolboy who set down that a lie was "an abomination in the sight of the Lord, but a very present help in time of trouble," deserved marks of some sort for his wit and impudence; and the philosopher who tells us that "a lie connotes an assertion made with full consciousness of its untruth and in order to mislead" speaks in language that anyone can understand.

This brings us to consider the relationship of the sin of lying to the crime of perjury. Many things are morally wrong which the law does not recognise as crimes. Lying is one of these. There is no law against mere lying as such. Indeed, a lie may cause damage to someone who believes it and yet give to the injured person no right of action. Even after a man has taken an oath in the witness-box and tells a lie in giving his evidence he does not necessarily commit the crime of perjury. To commit perjury is not such a simple business as a man may think. There are very many liars in the land who never attain to the dignity of real perjury.

Hallam tells us that the Middle Ages were a terrible period for perjury and thinks that trial by combat was continued as being a more likely method of ascertaining truth than judicial litigation with lying witnesses. Considering the prevalence of perjury in those ages, it is the more curious that at Common Law it does not seem originally to have been an indictable offence. The evolution of the crime in our legal history is of considerable interest. The Star Chamber started punishing perjurers in the time of Henry VII, but it was not until the reign of Elizabeth that it was made a statutory offence. Our Anglo-Saxon ancestors and many succeeding generations relied wholly on the sanctity of the oath as a guarantee of truthful evidence. The gist of a legal oath is that the swearer calls upon the Almighty to inflict punishment upon him if he is false to his oath. Once a witness had kissed the Book it was hardly conceivable to our pious forbears that he would risk his immortal soul by telling a lie. If he did, it probably seemed to them wanting in piety to take the matter out of the divine jurisdiction by administering earthly penalties. Robert, King of France, perceiving how frequently men forswore themselves upon the relics of the saints and thinking less of perjury than sacrilege, caused an empty reliquary of crystal to be used that those who kissed it might incur less guilt in fact though not in intention.

But as time wore on practical experience convinced the rulers of the people that courts of justice were frequented by hard swearers to whom the sanction of divine vengeance was too remote a peril to influence their testimony, but whose minds and behaviour would probably be more directly affected by the pillory and the whipping-post, which, standing opposite the Court-house, had the salutary effect of concentrating the thoughts of the reckless upon the disadvantages of dishonest testimony.

With that love of compromise which is the characteristic of all our legislators we have retained the religious sanction of the oath whilst at the same time we have strengthened the hands of the magistrates in the punishment of perjury. It is strange to-day to read in our decisions upon matters relating to the acceptance of evidence upon oath of the pious efforts of the devout to shut out the testimony of citizens on account of their religious views. George Fox, Margaret Fell, and, in recent years, Charles Bradlaugh, were persecuted and refused justice in the sacred name of religion. To-day we reap the reward of their courage and honesty in a saner series of statutes relating to oaths and evidence. One cannot blame the judges for yielding in these matters to popular bigotry, for they had to administer the bigotry of the law. As late as 1863, when Mrs. Maden in a Lancashire County Court was not allowed to give evidence because she honestly stated her views on matters of religion, the ruling was upheld in the High Court. But Baron Bramwell, whilst accurately administering the law, pointed out that the judgment he was giving involved the absurdity of ascertaining Mrs. Maden's disbelief by accepting her own testimony on the subject and then ruling that she was a person incompetent to speak the truth.

The fact of the matter is that an honest person will try and tell the truth because he thinks it right to do so, and a dishonest person will lie because he thinks it will serve his interests. Oaths and superstitious practices have very little practical effect on the accuracy of testimony, and I doubt if they ever exercised the stupendous sanction that some minds attached to them. As Judge Chalmers used to say, if every witness betted sixpence with the Court that he would tell the truth and the Judge was allowed to decide whether he had won or lost, evidence would be more carefully given, the sporting instinct of the man in the street would be satisfied, and the Exchequer would not lose by it.

The psychology of perjury to-day is, I fancy, little affected by the administration of the oath. Probably the large majority of witnesses desire to speak the truth and come prepared to do so, but the path of the martyr is full of pitfalls. One of these is our Law of Evidence. We demand of our witness that he should speak the truth, the whole truth, and nothing but the truth, but as soon as he begins to tell us what someone has said to him about the subject which was certainly part of the "truth," we interrupt him rudely with the statement that it is not

" evidence." One of the first causes of inaccurate testimony is that a Court of Law falsely pretends to a witness that it requires " truth " when in fact it wants "evidence," which is another story altogether.

Sir James Fitzjames Stephen was the first lawyer to ask himself the question, " What is evidence ? " He determined to answer it scientifically, and he did so. He found at hand in scattered reports and in amorphous text-books a mass of confusion gathered together in the wrong place, and he set about to reduce this material to a reasoned statement of legal principles. For instance, he found a common statement that " hearsay is not evidence." You will remember Justice Stareleigh saying to Sam Weller, " You must not tell us what the soldier or any other man said ; it's not evidence." But this was not enough for Stephen's scientific mind, for the statement " hearsay is not evidence " assumed that someone knew what " evidence " was. But no one knew anything of the kind.

To put the matter in Stephen's own inimitable words : " I found that I was in the position of a person who having never seen a cat is instructed about them in this fashion : ' Lions are not cats, nor are tigers, nor are leopards, though you might be inclined to think they were.' Show me a cat to begin with and I at once understand what is meant by saying that a lion is not a cat and why it is possible to call him one. Tell me what evidence is and I shall be able to understand why you say that this and that class of facts is not evidence."

Stephen, therefore, for the first time set before us in a peptonised and palatable form the leading principles of our English Law of Evidence. He told us what facts we may or may not prove, how we may prove them, and what instruments are permitted to be used to prove different classes of fact. It is a highly arbitrary business having about as much relation to nature as the rules of chess. Still, there is a game of evidence, and some advocates learn its rules and play within them. But no layman can possibly know anything about them, nor are they understood by many estimable lawyers. Solicitors who draft affidavits for their clients to swear can never have studied Stephen's great work. Chancery Judges who read these affidavits and are apparently impressed by what the deponents say they are informed and credibly —or is it credulously ?—believe must have forgotten any principles of evidence that they ever learned. As Sir Horace Davey is reported to have said, " Evidence was an ' extra ' at Lincoln's Inn, and many students did not take it." But in the Common Law Courts, where oral evidence prevails, the laws of evidence are understood and acted upon, and the poor witness, struggling to pour forth the truth, the whole truth, and nothing but the truth, is mystified and hampered in his efforts by being constantly pulled up because the truth he is speaking is not " evidence."

This makes the layman naturally impatient. But he must remember that our law of evidence is based on a principle of protecting the citizens from the dangers of doubtful testimony. The lawyers who framed it understood enough of the psychology of perjury to know that witnesses and juries left to their own notions of relevance would be the unwitting authors of grave injustice. Lord

Chief Baron Gilbert, who wrote a book on the Law of Evidence in 1801, noted with pride " that liberal caution with which the subject as well in civil as in criminal prosecutions is protected from the admission of any sort of testimony either suspicious in its nature or partial in its tendency." It was in pursuance of these ends that our forefathers refused to allow either Mrs. Bardell or Mr. Pickwick to give evidence as being parties to the action their testimony would be necessarily partial. Even in our own day there was great difficulty in persuading lawyers to allow a prisoner to give evidence. But no ages and no nations agree what is the best evidence, though doubtless all legal systems strive to obtain it. Our French neighbours encourage their witnesses " to *parler d'abondance*, that is, to narrate uninterruptedly the circumstances to which their evidence relates." Hearsay, opinion, argument, and fact are thrown together and the judge and counsel ask questions about it, and finally the Bench read it all in documentary form and sort out that which is relevant to the issue.

This method is to us scarcely comprehensible. We demand rigid demonstration and have always had a strong preference for the written document over mere oral evidence. Yet in another age and country that great advocate Cicero said that for his part he preferred the plain testimony of a man of honour and integrity to written tables that might be the subject of corruption and alteration.

It is necessary to understand our legal view of evidence before we can appreciate the true inwardness of the crime of perjury. Perjury, you may suppose, is the crime of lying in the witness-box. Roughly, that is a description of the business that may pass muster. But not every lie spoken in the box is perjury. The lie must be an " evidence " lie, so to speak. The false oath must be material to the issue, and it must be uttered wilfully, deliberately, and with intent to deceive, and nothing short of that wickedness is punishable as perjury.

Mere carelessness, foolishness, or even recklessness, in offering testimony to the Court falls far short of the crime of perjury. With the exception of evidence given in the Divorce Court, where the authorities seem to follow the Roman Law of Tibullus " perjuria ridet amantum Jupiter," I am inclined to hold the view that the testimony given by the average citizen in the courts is singularly free from the taint of perjury. But if, on the other hand, you were to ask me whether, after a third of a century's experience of listening to sworn testimony in our courts, I was deeply impressed by the accuracy, reliability and truth of the daily round of evidence it has been my duty to consider, I should with sincere regret be bound to admit that the answer was in the negative.

Why should this be so ? Assuming an earnest desire to relate facts exactly as they occurred, why should human beings fail, as they undoubtedly do, to attain the ideal of truthful narration that they are honestly attempting ? It is only recently that such questions have been scientifically considered. The psychology of perjury, or now that we have got a clear legal view of the crime of perjury perhaps we should more accurately say " the psychology of erroneous testimony," is a very subtle affair. It is a branch of the psychology of memory, but I doubt if the modern philosophers Freud, Brill, Ernest Jones, and the rest of them can explain the whole matter to us, since it is not entirely an affair for scientists, and the legal practitioner can throw some light on the matter from his practical experience of the courts.

The older judges shook their heads at the depravity and recklessness of witnesses and hastily concluded that all men were liars. It never occurred to them that their own methods of eliciting evidence often gave rise to confusion and error in testimony. I remember well a wise and learned judge complaining of my Welsh countrymen that even when they spoke English well they demanded an interpreter, as he considered, for the purpose of evasion and deceit. I knew that he somewhat fancied his own knowledge of the French tongue, and I asked him whether if he were in a French court about to be cross-examined by M. Labori he would or would not demand an interpreter? He admitted that he would. However well you may speak a foreign tongue, testimony should be sought and given in the language in which the witness thinks.

I have often, therefore, marvelled to hear really good advocates examining and cross-examining witnesses from the street and the market-place in language and words which are entirely beyond their comprehension. It is well to understand and descend to the vernacular of the pavement if you want to obtain the truth from the man in the street.

One of my learned brethren found a place in legal anthologies through his thoughtless utterance in the trial of a tangled case between two costermongers about the possession of a donkey. At the lunch hour he nodded pleasantly to the litigants and said: "Now, my men, I'm going to have my lunch, and before I come back I hope you'll settle your dispute out of Court." On his return the plaintiff had a black eye and the defendant had a bloody nose, and the defendant said: "Well, your Honour, we've taken your Honour's advice; Jim's given me a damn good hiding, and I've given him back his donkey."

The methods of advocacy practised and permitted in many courts do not always make for accuracy. The very best advocate is not above luring his witness towards the answer he wishes to elicit by the doubtful expedient of the leading question. He remembers Bacon's foxy advice that "it is a good point of cunning for a man to shape the answer he would have in his own words and proposition," and perhaps considers that it would savour of impiety for a junior to overrule the considered judgment of a Lord Chancellor. There are still in existence, too, survivals of a bygone age who seek to cross-examine a witness as to character by asking him in robustious accents: "Whether he has left off beating his wife?" and fiercely demanding a straight answer, "Yes or No."

Splendid as much of our advocacy is and sound as are its ideals in general, we cannot honestly claim that the practice of it is always a perfect apparatus for producing, weighing, and measuring the truth. Indeed, one may almost sympathise with the county justice of the peace who, having heard the evidence of many witnesses and listened to the conflicting interpretations of opposing counsel, was so unsettled and perplexed that he exclaimed: "So help me God! I will never listen to evidence again!"

These practical difficulties in court, however, only touch the fringe of the matter, and, without being oneself a philosopher or capable at all of criticising the psychologists, the various theories of illusion and memory that they put forward certainly throw light on the everyday task in the law courts of unravelling the truth from the web of human testimony.

The idea of Freud and his disciple Brill seems to be that, setting aside forgetfulness caused by organic brain trouble, a human being's so-called forgetting may be ultimately reduced to two causes; first, that he really did not wish to remember what he claims to have forgot; secondly, that he either never knew it or that he never considered it important enough to know. They think that there is an unconscious wish in all of us to eliminate what seems to us a shortcoming or what we regard as unpleasant. For the same reason we lose things we dislike, like umbrellas, since forgetting is proved to be founded on a motive of displeasure. Certainly most of us would agree with Brill that "we are more apt to mislay letters containing bills than cheques." Darwin noticed this tendency in himself, and, being a scientist of unswerving honesty, he followed a golden rule, namely, that whenever he came across a published thought opposed to the general results of his investigations or against the trend of his theory, he made a memorandum of it without fail and at once, for he says: "I had found by experience that such facts and thoughts were far more apt to escape from the memory than favourable ones."

This theory of forgetting is a very attractive one, and this natural tendency to " push into the unconscious " anything of unpleasant association throws considerable light upon the cause of error in human testimony. It accounts for many false reminiscences by apparently decent persons of having already paid bills or not having ordered goods still unpaid for. Everyone, too, is constantly practising psycho-analysis on his neighbour of whom it is easy and perhaps pleasant to remember evil, but of himself a man only remembers what is pleasing. Hence arise many family and neighbourly disputes where the evidence has all the outward appearance of perjury, but where, if the philosophers are right, the dispute is based on the fact that the Plaintiff and Defendant have each " pushed into the unconscious " all their own naughty doings and sayings.

I must confess that since I have known of this theory it accounts in a measure for many curiosities of testimony. I remember recently listening with surprise to the evidence of a professional man of the highest honour who was defendant in a running-down case. He was driving a car and turned out of the high road on the right-hand side at considerable speed, cutting the corner which was a blind corner. Another car coming down the lane on his proper side, in order to avoid a collision, swerved to his right. The defendant made the same manœuvre, and the crash came on the left-hand side of the lane. There was no doubt, from independent evidence and the wheel marks, that the cause of the accident was the cutting of the corner by the defendant, but he had ended up on his proper side of the lane and stoutly maintained that he had made a wide circuit to enter the lane on the left side and was surprised to see the plaintiff swerve across the road towards him. Directly after the accident he was busy helping the plaintiff, who was injured, and he never examined the wheel marks himself. He had no interest in the case whatever, as he was fully insured.

Now, throughout his evidence the witness contended that he had not cut the corner. He had a distinct memory to the contrary, but the true fact was beyond doubt. According to Freud, he must have " pushed into the unconscious " the memory of cutting the right-hand corner, and on the basic fact of finding himself on his proper side when the collision took place built up a " false reminiscence " of making a wide left-hand turn, lured to that conclusion by a common desire to remember righteous actions.

There is a great deal of " pushing into the unconscious " done by witnesses in running-down cases, but I do not think that alone accounts for all the erroneous testimony with which this class of case is too frequently encumbered. Talking over the matter with others and repeating the story to different hearers has a tendency to dilute the truth of the original. " The most frequent source of false memory," said James in his " Principles of Psychology," " is the accounts we give to others of our own experiences. Such accounts we almost always make both more simple and more interesting than the truth. We quote what we should have said or done rather than what we really said or did, and in the first telling we may be fully aware of the distinction. But ere long the fiction expels the reality from memory and reigns in its stead alone."

Professor Swift, of Washington University, makes the startling statement that " experiments have proved that in general when the average man reports events or conversations from memory and conscientiously believes that he is telling the truth, about one-fourth of his statements are incorrect, and this tendency to false memory is the greater the longer the time since the original experience." Auto-suggestion plays a great part in the machinery of testimony. Pondering over details which one feels must have happened and trying to recall whether they did really happen usually, says the Professor, ends in recollection.

To auto-suggestion one must add, perhaps, auto-attorney-suggestion. In nearly every running-down case there is the enthusiastic corner man who was standing outside the "Red Lion" and having plenty of time to discuss the matter with the intelligent clerk who is taking his proof, is duly talked into the belief that he has observed a condition of things which it is to the interest of the party calling him to prove. He is not really dishonest, but weak and imaginative and vain of his importance as a witness. Psychology teaches that if you tell a human being something and repeat it often enough, he finally accepts it, and as he continually repeats it, even as a possible fact, it ends by becoming firmly fixed in his mind. Then he believes he saw or heard it all. There is also the human instinct to take sides, and the knowledge, perhaps, that a day's pay depends on winning the case, and all these matters are apt to colour the casual testimony of the corner man. It is this class of witness which reacts most readily to skilful advocacy. Under the winnowing fan of cross-examination the chaff of his testimony is readily blown away, and if there is any grain left its weight is easily appraised.

And Professor Swift, whose pleasant volume, "Psychology and the Day's Work," every practitioner whose daily work lies in the courts should carry alongside "Roscoe" in his blue bag, has made some delightful experiments in the psychology of testimony and rumour which bear out my optimistic belief that the microbe of perjury is not the main cause of false evidence. Indeed, I trust that I have made it clear that the popular notion that Courts of Justice are constantly misled by wicked and abandoned perjurers and suborners conspiring to subvert the ends of Justice is a myth. There are such criminals, of course, men like Titus Oates and Arthur Orton and many lesser scoundrels who, not having the fear of God before their eyes, but being moved and seduced by the instigation of the Devil, deliberately enter the court with falsehood in their hearts and lies on their lips. But the bulk of erroneous testimony in the law courts is not perjury, but mere human frailty and incompetence common to all mankind.

Each individual is convinced that he is an accurate observer, and when a man tells you that he has seen a thing with his own eyes, he is offended if you do not at once accept his statement as evidence of a fact. A person who believes in spiritualism and attends séances will tell you of something he has "seen with his own eyes" when he is recounting a stale and common conjuring trick that has been exposed and explained time and again. In the eighties Mr. S. J. Davey made an elaborate series of experiments in slate-writing. He learned most of the slate mediums' conjuring tricks and himself held a number of successful séances. These were described by many honest folk who related what they "saw with their own eyes," and Mr. Davey, in a series of notes, shows how their testimony is inaccurate and useless. His long and interesting paper will be found in Vol. 4 of the "Proceedings of the Psychical Research Society," and is a very interesting study of the frailty of human testimony. It must be admitted that the trickery of good slate-writing was by no means easy to detect, and many of the mediums were very clever at it. Since Mr. Davey's paper the spirits no longer write on slates and content themselves with vaguer and more indirect methods of communication.

Professor Swift relates a very interesting experiment in human observation that he carried out with his psychology class at Washington. The regular work of the class was in progress and one of the students was reading a paper, when suddenly before the eyes of the students the following scene which had been carefully rehearsed was enacted. An altercation was heard in the corridor, then the door burst open, and four students, two young men and two young women, dashed into the room. Miss R. immediately after entering dropped on the floor a parcel containing a brick. K. flourished a large yellow banana as though it were a pistol. The professor rose as if to protest and dropped a cracker on the floor which went off with a bang. H. fell back crying, " I'm shot," and was caught by Miss T. They then hurried out, Miss R. picking up the parcel. The scene lasted thirty seconds.

The twenty-nine students of the class, who were considerably frightened, were now told that the scene was made to order and asked to write out their evidence of what they had observed. Three of the actors were actual members of the class, and Miss R. was a prominent senior of the college well-known to the students.

The analysis of the evidence gives very startling results. Of the twenty-nine " witnesses," only three knew that four persons entered the room. These three recognised that there were two young men and two young women. Many described the incursion as that of " a mob " or " a crowd." The evidence of identity was extraordinarily weak. Seven students recognised three, eleven recognised two, seven recognised one, and four recognised none. Yet all the actors were persons they met every day.

No less than eight persons identified individuals who were not there, and the identification by clothing was either so general as to be worthless or, where details were given, they were generally found to be inaccurate. Only one witness spoke to the brown-paper parcel ; no one saw Miss R. pick it up, though six saw someone pick it up and five of these said it was Miss T., whilst the others said it was H. Several students saw the flash of the pistol, and one young man wrote " they were attempting to hold back a man with long black hair." This must have referred to H., whose hair was, in fact, short.

The whole of Professor Swift's masterly analysis of the evidence and the psychological causes of the erroneous testimony should be studied in his own pages; but the value of the experiment to lawyers is that here we have before us the kind of raw material of evidence that is ultimately produced as a highly manufactured article, carded, dyed, and woven into a coherent piece of goods to be displayed with forensic decoration before judges and juries.

Had this little drama been a real crime very few of the witnesses' testimony was worth much, even immediately after the sight was fresh in their minds. Most of the witnesses had some indefinite, vague idea of what they had seen, yet after a few examinations by lawyers and police, human vanity and the desire to be in the picture would have suggested to the minds of these witnesses a large number of details which they would have gradually talked about and thought about until they came to believe in them as honest memories of facts.

In many running-down cases, where there is seldom any reason for any outside observer to be watching the vehicles before the actual crash startles the attention of all the bystanders, I am convinced that if we could get the first-hand memories of the witnesses we should receive the same class of vague, indefinite testimony that Professor Swift obtained from his students. In listening to evidence and trying to value its worth it is very important to endeavour to try and get back to the first picture in the mind of the witness and, if possible, subtract the suggested accretions from the original observations. Sometimes this is quite easy to do. I have several times heard a witness detail the movements of two vehicles for several moments before the collision, and later on, in answer to some indirect question, drop out the statement: "I turned round directly I heard the crash." This dates the moment when he was first in a position to give testimony. All his former statements are the result of suggestion. He honestly believes now that he saw these things, but of course he did not. That is a simple example of the process of eliminating false reminiscences; it is generally far more difficult and complicated, but Professor Swift's experiment is a warning to lawyers and judges of the necessity for a very watchful observation of human testimony.

I am glad to know myself, and I hope I have convinced my fellow-citizens, that the crime of perjury is a rare one in our courts and that most of the errors of testimony are due to defective observation, false reminiscences, the deflecting influence of suggestion, and the pleasures of imagination. Very often, too, the "wish to believe" is a strong factor in bringing about false testimony. How many English citizens "knew a friend" who had seen those splendid hordes of Russians passing through the country with the snow on their boots in midnight trains at the beginning of the war! It would be harsh to call such legends perjuries.

When mankind understands more fully and scientifically the real causes of error in human testimony which the professors have only in recent years begun to study scientifically, we shall be able to set about amending our ways and checking our bias and imagination and shunning the perils of undue suggestion. As creative evolution removes the *homo sapiens* of the future yet further away from his Neanderthal ancestors, we may hope that he will gradually eliminate all undesirable elements from his sworn testimony in the courts so that the judges of the future may have simpler and less anxious tasks.

Chapter VII : *Concerning Whistler v. Ruskin**

FRIENDLY chance threw in my way an old brief. What a vast amount of biographical and social history lies hidden in these foolscap folios tipped on to the solicitors' slag heap after the fires of litigation are burnt out and forgotten. What would we give, for instance, for Mr. St. John's brief in Hampden's case with the Defendant's own suggestions of the line to be taken by his advocate, or for Brougham's brief in Queen Caroline's case, or Campbell's brief in "Norton v. Melbourne." The true story of many a *cause célèbre* is never made manifest in the evidence given or in the advocates' orations, but might be recovered from these old papers when the dust of ages has rendered them immune from scandal.

The title of this particular brief is : "1877 W. No. 818. In the High Court of Justice, Queen's Bench Division. Whistler v. Ruskin. Brief on behalf of the Defendant. The Attorney-General, with you Mr. C. Bowen." I was deeply interested in this libel action at the time, as my father, Serjeant Parry, appeared with Mr. Petheram for

* The author gratefully acknowledges the kind permission of Miss R. Birnie Philip, the executrix of Mr. Whistler, and Mr. Alexander Wedderburn, K.C., the executor of Mr. Ruskin, to make use of the documents hitherto unpublished which are quoted in this essay.

the Plaintiff and ultimately wrested from Sir John Holker the glorious victory of a farthing damages.

The unfortunate dispute which brought these two great ones into the squalid purlieus of Westminster Hall was not based upon any mean personal antagonism, but was a passing form of the eternal quarrel between those who worship the art of personal impression and those who demand a literary inspiration—a picture with a story. Could it have been tried before a tribunal of " amateurs " eager to give ear to the earnest pleading of the litigants good might have come of the contest, but before Baron Huddlestone and a Middlesex jury who cared for none of these things the trial was a sorry farce.

The trouble began in this way. Ruskin was at the zenith of his fame as an art critic and had adopted the public rôle of prophet. He was wont to attack all and sundry with a savage merriment which even his best friends at times resented. The story goes that he wrote to a friend hoping that a fierce criticism published by him on his friend's picture would make no difference in their friendship. To which his friend had the wit to reply, " Dear Ruskin—Next time I meet you I shall knock you down, but I hope it will make no difference in our friendship."

In his own circle this kind of thing did not matter, but Whistler was not of the circle. Twelve years before Swinburne had asked Ruskin to come with Burne-Jones and himself to Whistler's studio, but the visit was never made. " I wish you could accompany us," he writes. " Whistler, as any artist worthy of his rank must be, is of course desirous to meet you and to let you see his immediate work. As (I think) he has never met you, you will see that his desire to have it out with you face to face must spring simply from knowledge and appreciation of your works." The prophet of Herne Hill was not inclined to come down into the studio and "have it out" with the apostle of a new gospel and the men never met.

In the year 1877 Ruskin was writing his letters to working men which he entitled "Fors Clavigera." The libel Whistler complained of appeared in Letter 79, and is dated "Herne Hill, June 18th, 1877." That Ruskin ever thought of or intended to injure Whistler personally is unthinkable. If you read the whole letter it is clear that the very mention of Whistler was almost accidental. He was striving to teach the lesson that true co-operation was not a policy of privileged members combining for their own advantage, but that we must "do the best we can for all men." This leads him to consider whether under present conditions any sort of Art is at all possible, and he arrives at the characteristic conclusion that it is not. Music he finds is possible, and that is because "our music has been chosen for us by our masters, and our pictures have been chosen by ourselves." If someone like Charles Hallé could guide us in our choice of pictures, as he does in music, all would be well.

This of necessity brings him to the recent opening of the Grosvenor Gallery by Sir Coutts Lindsay, and giving him credit for good intentions he dismisses him lightly with the phrase "that he is at present an amateur both in art and shop-keeping." He then proceeds to tell his working-men readers that the work of his friend Burne-Jones "is the only art work in England which will be received by the future as 'classic' of its kind, the best that has been or could be," and goes on to pronounce this final decree upon his pictures: "I *know* that these will be immortal as the best things the mid-nineteenth century could do."

This first exhibition of the Grosvenor Gallery was a loan exhibition, and considerable prominence was given to Whistler's nocturnes, including the "Falling Rocket" and "Old Battersea Bridge." Whistler himself had designed a frieze for one of the galleries, and he was treated as an artist worthy of serious consideration. The very fact of this being done in a gallery where his friend Burne-Jones's masterpieces are displayed excites Ruskin to a fit of uncontrollable anger, and with little attention to the context he concludes his panegyric of Burne-Jones with an almost irrelevant attack on Whistler. Nothing is said to the working men he is writing for as to why the pictures he dislikes are bad or what it is that is wrong about them. The paragraph suddenly introduces Whistler to an audience that probably knew little or nothing about him in the following terms:

"For Mr. Whistler's own sake no less than for the protection of the purchaser, Sir Coutts Lindsay ought not to have admitted works into the gallery in which the ill-educated conceit of the artist so nearly approached the aspect of wilful imposture. I have seen and heard much of Cockney impudence before now; but never expected to hear a coxcomb ask two hundred guineas for flinging a pot of paint in the public's face."

Time has shown that from the shop-keeper's point of view Sir Coutts Lindsay knew more about his business than Ruskin supposed, and the money taunt in the libel, which was wholly outside a critic's jurisdiction, gave an air of malice to the paragraph that was most unfortunate. In so far as money talks in questions of Art the prices of Whistler's nocturnes have dismissed the criticism of Ruskin as futile and unsound. " Battersea Bridge," for instance, the Blue and Silver Nocturne, which was produced at the trial, was ultimately purchased by the National Art Collection Fund for two thousand guineas, presented to the nation, and hangs in the National Gallery.

If the libel had remained interred in the pages of " Fors Clavigera," it would possibly never have reached Whistler's ears. The curious côterie who read Ruskin's monthly letters cared little and knew less about " nocturnes in blue and gold " and " arrangements in black." The magazine was not one that found its way into clubs and the drawing-rooms of Society. But the passage was too piquant to remain in obscurity. It was copied into other papers and repeated with a chuckle by the Tadpoles and Tapers of artistic society.

In Pennell's admirable life of the artist, where the circumstances of the trial are very faithfully dealt with, we are told that Boughton remembered Whistler chancing on the criticism in the smoking-room at the Arts Club.

" It is the most debased *style* of criticism I have had thrown at me yet," Whistler said.

" Sounds rather like libel," Boughton suggested.

" Well—that I shall try and find out," Whistler replied.

It is a thousand pities that such an idea was ever suggested to Whistler, but it is more than probable it would have come to him spontaneously. The two men stood for opposite ideals. The public at that date regarded Whistler as a mountebank and Ruskin as an English institution infallible and almost sacred in the domain of Art. There was some excuse for these erroneous estimates. But here, from Whistler's point of view, was an opportunity to exterminate a prophet and destroy a false doctrine, and when the challenge was made the old warrior in Ruskin scented the battlefield and the destruction of poisonous dragons.

On July 21st it was stated in the " Athenæum " that Whistler intended to bring an action against Mr. Ruskin " on account of opinions expressed with regard to the artist, his works, or both, we do not gather which." On July 28th the Writ was issued, and the pleadings were closed on December 11th.

Ruskin wrote at once to Burne-Jones full of the early enthusiasm of the joyful litigant :

" It's mere nuts and nectar to me, the notion of having to answer for myself in Court—and the whole thing will enable me to assert some principles of art economy which I've never got into the public's head by writing but may get sent over all the world vividly in a newspaper report or two."

It has been suggested that the libel might possibly be accounted for by Ruskin's morbid mental condition, but his letter does not bear any trace of depression. Moreover, he had penned a similar attack on Whistler in an Oxford Lecture on Tuscan Art in 1873, in which he had said :

" I never saw anything so impudent on the walls of any

exhibition in any country as last year in London. It was a daub professing to be a 'harmony in pink and white' (or some such nonsense); absolute rubbish and which had taken about quarter of an hour to scrawl or daub—it had no pretence to be called painting. The price asked for it was two hundred and fifty guineas."

It is probable that Whistler never saw or heard of this passage, or his legal advisers would have been told of it. But it shows that Ruskin's attack was not a sudden outburst of momentary irritation, but was deliberate and intentional.

Ruskin would undoubtedly have enjoyed testifying from the witness-box. But alas! for the vanity of human wishes; long before the case came on Ruskin's serious illness rendered it impossible for him to risk the excitement of appearing in court. It is only fair to Whistler to remember that he extended the time of hearing whenever he was requested to do so, and his advisers were naturally anxious that Ruskin should go into the box to be cross-examined.

Meanwhile the prophet returned to Brantwood and prepared a characteristic memorandum of his views on the particular case and a general dissertation on the ethics of criticism, which we find attached to Sir John Holker's brief. Having set out that the function of all good critics is "to recommend Authors of merit to public attention and to prevent authors of demerit from occupying it," Ruskin tells his counsel that the main strength of his life has been spent in the praise of unappreciated artists. "But," he continues, "the Bench of Honourable Criticism is as truly a seat of judgment as that of Law itself and its verdicts though usually kinder must sometimes be no less stern. It has ordinarily been my privilege to extol but occasionally my duty to condemn the works of living painters. But no artist has ever yet been suspected of purchasing my praise, and this is the first attempt that has been made through the instrumentality of the British Law to tax my blame."

Sir John Holker underlines this passage with the pencil of approval.

The Defendant then sets out his view of the libel: "I do not know," he writes, "the sense attached legally to the word 'libel,' but the sense rationally attaching to it is that of a false description of a man's person, character or work made wilfully for the purpose of injuring him.

"And the only answers I think it necessary to make to the charge of libel brought against me by the Plaintiff are, first that the description given of his work and character is accurately true as far as it reaches, and secondly that it was calculated, so far as it was accepted, to be extremely beneficial to himself and still more to the public. In the first place the description given of him is absolutely true. It is my constant habit while I praise without scruple to weigh my words of blame in every syllable. I have spoken of the Plaintiff as ill-educated and conceited because the very first meaning of education in an artist is that he should know his true position with respect to his fellow-workmen and ask from the public only a just price for his work. Had the Plaintiff known either what good artists gave habitually of labour to their pictures or received contentedly of pay for them, the price he set on his own productions would not have been coxcombry but dishonesty."

In this purely commercial question of price Ruskin was clearly wrong and entirely out of his element. As the market has turned out, Whistler was at that date offering his wares at absurdly cheap prices, and if Ruskin had gone into the witness-box he would have been a tempting subject for cross-examination on the question why an art critic should disturb his mind about the price asked for a picture. There was only one picture of Whistler's for sale at the Grosvenor Gallery, the others were loaned, and the fact that Ruskin fastened on the one priced exhibit to attack the artist was some evidence of unfairness if not malice.

Having scornfully disposed of Whistler's musical descriptions of his pictures as mere evidence of quackery, Ruskin then proceeds to lay down the only true gospel of Art.

"The standard which I gave thirty years ago," he repeats with pride, "for estimate of the relative value of pictures, namely, that their preciousness depended ultimately on the clearness and justice of the ideas they contained and conveyed, has never been lost sight of by me since, and has been especially dwelt upon lately in such resistance as I have been able to offer to the modern schools which conceive the object of Art to be ornament rather than edification."

He then continues to enlighten counsel on the degradation of trade and art in the nineteenth century, reminding him that in the good old days of flourishing trade and art "the dignity of operative, merchant, and artist was held alike to consist in giving each in their several functions good value for money and a fair day's work for a fair day's wage. . . . I have now long enough endeavoured much to my own hindrance to vindicate from the impatient modern some respect for the honesties of commerce and the veracities of art which characterised the simplicity of his uncivilised forefathers. I contentedly henceforward leave the public of this brighter day to appease the occasional qualms that may trouble the liberty of their conscience and the latitude of their taste with philosophy that does nobody any good and criticism that does no one any harm."

Holker and Bowen must have thanked their stars that their outspoken client was safe at Brantwood and they were at liberty to make use of as much or as little of his instructions as they thought right. Bowen had already given him an intimation of the course the jury were likely to take and instinctively notices that the sting of the libel was in the unwise and unnecessary introduction of the price asked for the picture.

" Most people of educated habits of mind," he writes, " are well aware of the infinite importance of having works of art or alleged works of art freely and severely criticised by skilled and competent critics. But Mr. Ruskin must not expect that he will necessarily find Juries composed of persons who have any knowledge or sympathy with Art. It would, for example, be hopeless to try to convince a Jury that Mr. Ruskin's view of Mr. Whistler's performance was right : they never could or would decide on that. They would look to the language used rather than to the provocation, and their sympathies would rather lean to the side of the man who wanted to sell his pictures than to the side of the outspoken critic whose criticism interfered with the sale of a marketable commodity. I think, therefore, that Mr. Ruskin, whose language about Mr. Whistler in 'Fors Clavigera' is exceedingly trenchant and contemptuous, must not be surprised if he loses the verdict. I should rather expect him to do so."

One of the main themes of Ruskin's article being the praise of the work of Burne-Jones and the dispraise of the work of his fellow-artist Whistler, friendship and good taste ought to have prevented Ruskin from inviting Burne-Jones to appear for him as a witness.

But that was not Ruskin's way. In any contest in which he was engaged he at once found himself fighting on the side of righteousness against the Evil One and conducted the battle with Old Testament energy, enthusiasm, and even want of chivalry.

On November 2, 1878, he writes to Burne-Jones:

"I gave your name to the blessed lawyers as chief of men to whom they might refer for anything which in their wisdom they can't discern unaided concerning me. But I commanded them in no wise and for no cause whatsoever to trouble or tease you."

As a matter of fact the "blessed lawyers" were given to understand that Mr. Burne-Jones was desirous to give evidence and that Leslie, Richmond and Marks among the Royal Academicians would wish to do so also. The worldly lawyers shrewdly suggested that you cannot expect artist to give evidence against artist, and hinted that no artist ever did approve of criticism. In this they turned out to be right, and Burne-Jones was the only one who showed little backwardness in coming forward. The others refused to be mixed up in the quarrel.

In after years Burne-Jones himself regretted that he had felt obliged in loyalty to his friend to accept the invitation. " The whole thing," he wrote, " was a hateful affair and nothing in a small way annoyed me more—however, as I had to go I spoke my mind and I try not to think of it all more than I can help." Looking back on the affair, he was sincerely sorry that it had happened. " I wish," he said to a friend, " that trial thing hadn't been; so much I wish it and I wish Whistler knew that it made me sorry—but he would not believe."

For the artist in him loved Whistler's colour and admired his technique, though he was on Ruskin's side in the essentials of the artistic quarrel. Ruskin was his chief and his friend, and called upon to take action he was at the moment very ready for the fray and sat down and wrote very frankly and at length his view of the position, which we find set out in the brief.

" The point and matter," he writes, " seems to be this: that scarcely anybody regards Whistler as a serious artist—for years past he has so worked the art of brag that he has succeeded in a measure amongst the semi-artistic part of the public, but amongst artists his vanities and eccentricities have been a matter of joke of long standing. . . . It is a matter of jest, but a matter of fact that he has been ceaseless in all company for years past in depreciating the work of all artists living or dead and without any shame at all proclaiming himself as the only painter who has lived."

As Whistler used to say to his devoted disciples: "You must be occupied with the Master, not with yourselves." Typical, too, was his rebuke to Oscar Wilde, who had suggested that when together their talk was about themselves: "No, no, Oscar, you forget when you and I are together we never talk about anything except me."

Burne-Jones knew his man well when he said:

"If he were asked if this were the case he would not care to deny it, for he has a perfect estimate of the value of this trumpeting, knowing that there will always be some to be staggered by it and some to believe it. He has never yet produced anything but sketches more or less clever, often stupid, sometimes sheerly insolent—but sketches always. For all artists know that the difficulty of painting lies in the question of completion, thousands can sketch cleverly, amateurs often as adroitly as artists. The test is finish; in finishing the chance of failure increases in overwhelming proportion. To complete and not to lose the first vigour, that is what all painters have always set before themselves without exception. That Whistler should be an incomplete artist on such terms concerns himself alone, but that for years past he should have been proclaiming this incompleteness with all his power of speech to be the only thing worth attaining concerns Art itself and all artists. And Mr. Ruskin's forty years of striving to raise the ideal of his country's skill would have ended tamely if he could have quietly let pass such an exhibition as Mr. Whistler's theory and practice. . . . And I think Mr. Ruskin's language is justified on the grounds of the scandal that this violent puffing of what is at best a poor performance brings upon

Art. I am sure that an ordinary intelligent person would think that a bad joke was being put upon him if he were asked to admire as a serious work of art the sort of picture condemned by Mr. Ruskin.

"It needs no length of explanation for the causes that should for a time give Mr. Whistler a little notoriety, but if anyone caring as Mr. Ruskin does for the question of Art and looking with any reverence on the works handed down to us could think this meaningless scribbling should be looked upon as real Art for admiration and reward I think he might lay his pen down and never write again, for Art would be at an end."

Holding these views about Whistler the man, it is good to remember that Burne-Jones in giving his evidence paid a fair tribute to Whistler's skill as an artist and did not go further than endorse Ruskin's principle that good workmanship was essential to a good picture.

After he had given his evidence Ruskin wrote him a characteristic letter of thanks:

"Brantwood, *November* 28.

"I'm very grateful to you for speaking up, and Arthur (Severn) says you looked so serene and dignified that it was a sight to see. I don't think you will be sorry hereafter that you stood by me, and I shall be evermore happier in my secure sense of your truth to me and to good causes, for there was more difficulty in your appearing than in anyone else's, and I'm so glad you looked nice and spoke so steadily."

Whistler had the same difficulty that Ruskin had in getting his artist friends to come forward and champion his cause in court. The following letter sent by Mr. Anderson Rose to my father, Serjeant Parry, shows how eager he too was to make a brave show on the day of the fight:

"21 *Novr.*, 1878.

"DEAR ROSE,

"Another view of the case and a further note for Serjt. Parry—First I am *known* and *always have been known* to hold an independent position in Art and to have had the Academy opposed to me. That *is* my position, and this would explain away the appearance of Academicians against me—and offering to paint my pictures in five minutes! and I fancy it would be a good thing for Parry to take the initiative and say this,—and prepare the Jury for all Academic demonstration.—Again I don't stand in the position of the *popular* picture maker with herds of admirers—my art is quite apart from the usual stuff furnished to the mass and *therefore* I necessarily have *not* the *large number of witnesses!*—In defending me it would be bad policy to try and make me out a different person than the well-known Whistler—besides I think more is to be gained by sticking to that character.

"However here are one or two more men to be subpœnaed:

"*Richard Holmes*—Queen's Librarian—Windsor.

"*Reid.*—The print room—British Museum.

"*Charles Keen* (sic) 11, Queen's Road West—Chelsea.

"*James Tissot.*—17 Grove End Road, St. John's Wood. Though I don't think that Whistler ought to have many more than Boehm and Albert Moore:—

"What would you think of the Revd. Haweis? You

know he *preached* about the beauty of the Peacock Room —and I have his printed sermon—it is a perfect poem of praise :—he could be subpœnaed to swear to what he had preached!

" Could you subpœna Prince Teck? to swear that he thought the Peacock Room a great piece of Art?

" Good night—

" J. Mc'N. WHISTLER.

" Another thing I have just heard—The other side is not at all so cocksure as they pretend to be! It's a game of bluff, my dear Rose :—and we mustn't be bounced out!"

Pennell says that Whistler " thought at first that the artists would be on his side and would combine with him to drive the false prophet out of the temple," but " they all sneaked away except Albert Moore."

Charles Keene, whose work Whistler greatly admired, was among those who with one accord made excuse:

" Whistler's case against Ruskin," he writes, " comes off, I believe, on Monday. He wants to subpœna me as a witness as to whether he is (as Ruskin says) an impostor or not. I told him I should be glad to record my opinion, but begged him to do without me if he could. They say it will be most likely settled on the point of law, but if the evidence is adduced it will be the greatest 'lark' that has been known for a long time in the Courts."

Even Whistler's friends could not take him or his case very seriously. The real quarrel between Whistler and Ruskin as to the literary or decorative basis of Art was, of course, quite incomprehensible to a judge and jury, and the personal dispute between the two was bound, as Keene saw, to be something of a " lark." That was the pity of it.

At the trial itself Whistler certainly enjoyed himself. He was more than a match for the Attorney-General, and his famous reply to one of his questions has passed into history:

" Can you tell me," asked Sir John Holker, " how long it took you to knock off that nocturne ? "

" Two days," replied Whistler.

" The labour of two days, then, is that for which you ask two hundred guineas ? "

" No. I ask it for the knowledge of a lifetime."

It is curious that Holker, with a hundred guineas on his brief, should have risked such a foolish gibe against so clever a man, but I fancy the whole of his cross-examination was really directed to allow the witness to exhibit to the jury his conceit and self-infatuation, qualities which, coupled with his eccentric appearance, were bound to tell in mitigation of damages, which was all that Holker expected.

Rossetti, Albert Moore, and W. G. Wills gave evidence for the Plaintiff. Burne-Jones, Frith, and Tom Taylor —a curious trinity—testified for Ruskin.

That Ruskin should have called Frith as a witness was remarkable. An amusing incident occurred in his cross-examination when he concurred in the description of Turner's snowstorm at sea as seen from the Harwich boat, as " soapsuds and whitewash," and observed that his latest pictures were as insane as the people who admired them.

Ruskin himself has told us how years ago poor Turner at his father's house sat in a corner murmuring to himself, " Soapsuds and whitewash," again and again. " At last," says Ruskin, " I went to him asking him why he minded what they said. Then he burst out, ' Soapsuds and whitewash ! What would they have ? I wonder what they think the sea is like ? I wish they had been in it ! ' "

Ruskin might have remembered this incident before he fell foul of the " Rocket at Cremorne."

The details of the trial are well reported in Pennell's " Life of Whistler," and the artist printed his own inimitable account of the proceedings. The result was a farthing damages, and Baron Huddlestone ordered each party to pay their own costs. Ruskin's admirers subscribed his costs, and Whistler wrote to his solicitors suggesting that he too should have a subscription, adding with undiminished humour, " and in the event of a subscription I would willingly contribute my mite."

Ruskin, who was in broken health, took the verdict very seriously and wrote to Liddell to resign his Art Professorship at Oxford on November 28th :

" The result of the Whistler trial," he says, " leaves me no further option. I cannot hold a chair from which I have no power of expressing judgment without being taxed for it by British Law."

Whistler, who, already on the verge of insolvency, was badly injured by the trial and its inconclusive result, solaced himself with pleasant epigrams at his opponent's expense, the best and worthiest of remembrance being perhaps the witty saying : " A life passed among pictures makes not a painter—else the policeman in the National Gallery might assert himself."

To the outer world the trial was a storm in a teapot—a trivial personal dispute between two great men, and the smaller fry chuckled to find that these giants could lose their temper and fling language at each other like men of commoner clay.

But to each individual it was a serious quarrel on a serious subject, though the disputants could not get judge, jury, or populace to understand it. The dispute remains undetermined and the riddle remains unsolved. Whether the Cave man and the child are really trying with soul and conscience to tell us the whole outward and inward truth of the subject etched on a bone or scrawled on a slate, or whether they are merely expressing decorative personal impressions of their own emotions about the subjects they deal with—that was roughly the cause of action between Whistler and Ruskin.

The British jury assessed the commercial importance of the proposition at a farthing, but to lovers of art it remains one of the deep, unanswered problems of the universe.

In the catalogue of the Pennell-Whistler collection in the Library of Congress at Washington there is an entry: "5. Complete Brief for the Plaintiff. Whistler. marked with Serjeant Parry's fee of thirty guineas." To that case has recently been added the "complete brief" of Sir John Holker. It is strange to think that these two sets of papers, once lying next each other on the desk in Westminster Hall, should come together again in such different surroundings. Once munitions of war in a fierce struggle for the supremacy of conflicting ideals, they rest for ever in their museum tomb across the seas within sound of the song of Hiawatha :

> " Buried was the bloody hatchet,
> Buried was the dreadful war-club,
> Buried were all war-like weapons,
> And the war-cry was forgotten."

Chapter VIII : *Concerning Mr. Justice Maule*

EULOGISTS of Sir William Henry Maule have sought to satisfy posterity that he was some kind of a great man ; but that was far from being the case. He was a learned judge—indeed, within the curtilage of the Courts all judges are *ex officio* learned judges—and by the courtesy of the Press the epithet obtains in obituary notices ; but he was not a great judge. He was certainly a shrewd judge and a studious scholar ; but his title to remembrance among the members of his profession is not that he was a great man, but rather that he was a great character. His very moderate success at the Bar has been attributed by friendly critics to a want of sycophancy. He was always "blowing up his attorney," and the wretched fellow rebelled. As a matter of hard fact, attorneys rather like being kicked and cuffed by their counsel—if he is a big enough man. Russell knew the secret of this ; but Maule was not a Russell.

On the Bench the pithy common sense of his legal decisions, though very recognisable to any who care to turn over the dry pages of " Clark and Finnelly " and " Manning and Granger," are long forgotten and overwhelmed in the memories and traditions of the wit and irony with which he illumined the dullest wrangles in the Common

Pleas or Exchequer. " An Irony," says an old writer, " is a nipping jeast or a speech that hath the honey of pleasantnesse in its mouth and a sting of rebuke in its taile." Maule was a master of irony. Had he only made equal use of his other abilities he might have been remembered as a considerable advocate or even a powerful judge ; but he had a gift which, in season or out of season, he was compelled to display—the gift of irony—and it is the echoes of these strange outbursts of his, coldly reported in careless memoirs or told with advantage over the mess table on circuit, that I have sought to collect and set down. For it is only in Mauleiana that you can get any true glimpse of Mr. Justice Maule.

There is a colourless book of Maule's early life written by a niece who can never, one suspects, have heard of uncle's wild flights of mockery and sarcasm. It portrays for you an industrious young man, a sort of legal curate, going through the blameless stages of a successful career. Of the early biographical material there displayed it is sufficient for our purpose to remember that Maule was born on the 25th of April, 1788, at Edmonton in Middlesex ; that his father was a respectable doctor ; that he was at school at his uncle's near Ealing, and afterwards commenced residence at Trinity College, Cambridge.

Greville was at the same school and remembers Maule's uncle as " an excellent scholar and a great brute." He also recalls a vivid picture of young Maule stimulated to further and better educational studies by being " suspended by the hair of the head while being well caned." It is notable that years afterwards Greville met Maule at a club, and went up to him where he was reading a paper to renew the friendship of old schooldays. Maule looked up, grunted at him that it was "too long ago to talk about," and retired into his newspaper. Whereupon Greville says very shrewdly: "So I set him down for a brute like his uncle and troubled him no further." This anecdote of his ill manners is more than probable. A man who rejoices to exhibit his gifts of sarcasm and ridicule at the expense of his fellow-men is bound to have his pleasanter social traits somewhat blunted in the practice.

Two further things may be set down by way of introduction. Maule was beyond doubt a very learned mathematician. He was a personal friend of Mr. Babbage, who extols Maule's deep knowledge of his own science. He and Babbage would play a game of mental chess with each other to while away the tedium of a coach journey—a feat not possible to men of ordinary powers of memory. It is interesting to remember that in Lewis Carroll, an ironist of a different type from Maule, we have another example of a deeply scientific mathematician revelling in the expression of ludicrous antiphrasis and quaint ridicule and mockage of commonplace humanity. Mr. Dodgson had a similar faculty of memory, and would amuse his sleepless nights going through a book or two of Euclid, the figures and letters of which he could visualise in the dark. At first blush the last man you would suspect of irony would be the mathematician. But it may be that the certitude that two and two make four, combined with some knowledge of the basic reasons why they make four, lures the scientist into the naughty, mocking pleasure of exhibiting those simple figures in phantom forms of three and five to the utter confusion of the homely dunces around him.

One of the uses of wit, says Dr. Isaac Barrow, is to "season matters otherwise distasteful or insipid with an unusual and thence grateful tang." This, no doubt, is the moral charter of the judicial humorist. But the judge should not forget his more menial duties in the exercise of his humour. With Maule it is safe to say that no solemnity of occasion ever stood between him and his "nipping jeast." This may be illustrated by the following well-authenticated story which has a real shudder in its humour.

A prisoner was found guilty of a sensational murder, and being asked in the usual way why sentence should not be passed upon him, exclaimed dramatically in a loud voice: "May God strike me dead, if I did it!"

There was a hushed silence throughout the crowded court. The spectators gazed at the prisoner in horror. Maule looked steadily in front of him and waited without a movement.

At length, after a pause of several moments, he coughed and began to address the prisoner in his dry, asthmatic voice as though he were dealing with some legal point that had been raised in the case: "Prisoner at the Bar, as Providence has not seen fit to interfere in your case, it now becomes my duty to pronounce upon you the sentence of death."

This he did with the usual solemnities. The really great humorist might have thought of the jest, of course, but he certainly would not have uttered it on such an occasion.

More easy to forgive is the harangue that he gave to poor Hall, the bigamist, without which no collection of Maule stories would be complete. It was the starting-point of the Divorce Act, and such marriage law reforms that we have since received date from Maule's ironical speech. The best account of it is in that charming volume of legal biography, Atlay's " Victorian Chancellors."

Hall was a labouring man convicted of bigamy and called up for sentence. Maule, in passing sentence, said that it did appear that he had been hardly used.

" I have indeed, my lord," called out poor Hall ; " it is very hard."

" Hold your tongue, Hall," quoth the judge, " you must not interrupt me. What I say is the law of the land which you in common with everyone else are bound to obey. No doubt it is very hard for you to have been so used and not be able to have another wife to live with you when Mary Ann had gone away to live with another man, having first robbed you ; but such is the law. The law in fact is the same to you as it is to the rich man ; it is the same to the low and poor as it is to the mighty and rich, and through it you alone can hope to obtain effectual and sufficient relief, and what the rich man would have done you should have done also, you should have followed the same course."

" But I had no money, my lord," exclaimed Hall.

" Hold your tongue," rejoined the Judge, " you should not interrupt me, especially when I am only speaking to inform you as to what you should have done, and for your good. Yes, Hall, you should have brought an action and obtained damages, which probably the other side would not have been able to pay, in which case you would have had to pay your own costs, perhaps a hundred or a hundred and fifty pounds."

"Oh, lord!" ejaculated the prisoner.

"Don't interrupt me, Hall," said Maule, "but attend. But even then you must not have married again. No; you should have gone to the Ecclesiastical Court and then to the House of Lords, where, having proved that all these preliminary matters had been complied with, you would then have been able to marry again! It is very true, Hall, you might say, 'Where was all the money to come from to pay for all this?' And certainly that was a serious question, as the expenses might amount to five or six hundred pounds while you had not as many pence."

"As I hope to be saved, I have not a penny—I am only a poor man."

"Well, don't interrupt me; that may be so, but that will not exempt you from paying the penalty for the felony you have undoubtedly committed. I should have been disposed to have treated the matter more lightly if you had told Maria the real state of the case and said, 'I'll marry you if you choose to take your chance and risk it,' but this you have not done."

And so the Judge gave Hall three months or, as some say, four. But that was because he had not told Maria all about it.

For my part, I do not trace any real sympathy for Hall in Maule's address; nor can I find that he ever showed any very kindly feelings for the men and women who came before him. To Maule the Court was a machine not to administer justice, but to declare the law and compel its due observation. It did not worry Maule that injustice was going to be done, and he laid down with unctuous pleasure that "it was much more important that a statute should receive its proper construction than that justice should be doled out to suit the circumstances of each particular case."

So high did he ride this hobby that his contemporaries credited him with the authorship of a new maxim, *Fiat jus ruat justitia*. But irony is often a just weapon, and Maule would sometimes use his gift by way of just rebuke.

A crowd of women had thronged the Court to listen to a case of an unpleasant character, and a witness hesitated to continue a certain part of his evidence in deference to feminine ears. Maule, who had already suggested that ladies should leave the Court, waved his hand blandly to the witness, saying, "Out with it! Out with it; the ladies don't mind it, and you needn't mind me."

Again, when Lord Chief Justice Wilde, on an appeal in a breach of promise case, took occasion to make a tirade against the present state of the law which allowed such an action at all, Maule in following opened his judgment by saying: "The question of what the law ought to be, having now been amply discussed by My Lord, I will now for my part consider what it really is." This bold rebuke of his chief was much admired at the time, though it is not to be supposed that it was seriously resented. Judges have from time immemorial been free to rebuke each other in a brotherly spirit, and doubtless the Lord Chief got his own back later on.

There are several excellent stories of his ironic advice

to juries, in some of which matters are made clear to them and light is thrown on the sophistries of learned counsel ; in others the shafts of wit wing their way high above the heads of the common citizens in the jury-box and fall useless to the ground.

Nothing can be better than his description of " some evidence "—a favourite last straw of counsel in a bad case. Counsel persists that there is " some evidence " to go to the jury, and the jury, hearing there is " some evidence," listen eagerly to the oration that seeks to magnify it into material for a verdict.

Maule said the last word on " some evidence " when he summed up to a jury thus : " Gentlemen, the learned counsel is perfectly right in law, there is some evidence upon that point ; but he's a lawyer and you are not, and you don't know what he means by ' some evidence.' So I'll tell you. Suppose there was an action on a bill of exchange and six people swore that they saw the defendant accept it, and six others swore they heard him say he should have to pay it, and six others knew him intimately and swore to his handwriting ; and suppose on the other side they called a poor old man who had been at school with the defendant forty years before, and had not seen him since, and he said he rather thought the acceptance was not his writing, why, there'd be *some* evidence that it was not. And that's what the learned counsel means in this case."

But if Maule was emphatic on the futility of " some evidence," he was very sound and clear—especially looking at the age in which he lived—on the danger of rejecting real evidence on some technical plea. A prisoner was charged with stealing pepper from the docks, and his counsel took the point that they had not proved the *corpus delicti*. Maule's common sense would not have this. " It is the *offence* you have to prove, not the *corpus delicti*. If," he continued, " a man go into the London Docks sober without means of getting drunk and comes out of one of the cellars very drunk, wherein are a million gallons of wine, I think that would be reasonable evidence that he had stolen some of the wine in that cellar, though you could not prove that any wine was stolen or any wine was missed."

How you could prove the *corpus delicti* specifically, when it was inside the prisoner, was too much for counsel to say.

That irony is not every man's food and that Maule cared on occasion for the display of his wit rather than the result of the trial before him is made clear by more than one mocking summing up which the common jury listened to with gaping but serious attention.

In the trial of a serious case of wounding with intent to do grievous bodily harm, the prisoner's counsel had sought to persuade the jury to find a verdict of a common assault, and Maule thought it sufficient to put the affair before them in the form, as he thought, of an absurdity. " It is quite true," he said, " what the counsel for the prisoner has told you, that if the prisoner did not intend to do grievous bodily harm he could not be convicted of that offence. If, therefore, you are of opinion that the ripping up of the prosecutor's belly so as to cause the bowels to protrude was done without the intent of doing him any bodily harm, you should acquit the prisoner of the aggravated, and find him guilty of a common assault ; but if you are of opinion that he had the intent to do grievous bodily harm, you should find him guilty of the greater offence."

When the jury found a verdict of common assault, history is silent as to how it was received by the judge.

Maule was not disliked by the abler members of the Bar who appeared before him ; but he was very impatient of anything like incompetence, or the assumption of ability not possessed. " I wish you would put your facts in some kind of order," he said to a confused and ill-prepared counsel. " Chronological order is one way and perhaps the best, but I am not particular ; any order you like—alphabetical order, if you prefer it."

Again, on circuit, a young counsel of great pretensions and high connection, who was prosecuting a thief, displayed, as Maule thought, a pompous and offensive manner which required that the conceit should be taken out of him. This, to Maule, was of far more immediate importance than the conviction of the guilty thief. Maule sat silent watching his young victim until the end of the case.

" Have you no more witnesses to call, sir ? " asked the Judge.

" No, my lord," replied counsel, in a tone that suggested that his lordship could see that for himself.

" Then your case is closed ? " asked Maule.

" Certainly, my lord," replied the counsel, somewhat puzzled and indignant at the Judge asking him again.

" Then, gentlemen of the jury," said Maule, turning round to them with a malicious cough, " you have only to acquit the prisoner, as no evidence has been given of the property in the article alleged to be stolen, and for aught that appears it might be the prisoner's own."

But though he would allow the acquittal of a guilty prisoner, for the purpose of punishing the incompetence of an offensive counsel, he was not always so harsh in his methods. Hawkins has a story of two young attorney's clerks fighting in chambers before Maule, who promptly decided against one of them. Thereupon as the unsuccessful one was leaving the room, he called Maule " a damned old fool." The shocked doorkeeper reported the matter to the Judge, who ordered the boy to be brought back. Looking over his desk at the pale and trembling clerk, he read him the following kindly rebuke: " I understand that in passing out of these chambers you called me 'a damned old fool.' I don't say you are wrong, my boy, for a moment; you may be right. I may be a damned old fool, but it would have been more polite if you had deferred the expression of your opinion until you were outside. You may now go."

In merrier vein was his reply to Alderson, the criminal counsel who, when defending a prisoner, had wound an eloquent address to the jury by declaring that his client was the victim of " a shameful, an infamous, I may say, a diabolical prosecution!"

" Gentlemen of the jury," began Maule in a thin, dry voice, " you are told that this is a diabolical prosecution, but, gentlemen, it is my duty to direct you that you must give the devil his due, and that can only be done by finding the defendant guilty." Then followed a cogent summing up, ending, as the Judge desired, in a verdict of guilty.

What the Judge Thought

It is never very wise to remind a judge that he has omitted this, that, or the other point, in his summing up. There is a good deal of original sin in the judicial person, and he often takes advantage of such an application by counsel to rub into the minds of the jury other matters that counsel by no means desired to call attention to. Maule was a very dangerous person to interfere with, and few counsel dared to do it. One more foolhardy than others was defending a Bible reader and Sunday-school teacher charged with a serious offence. A lot of evidence had been called to the man's character, but the direct evidence was overwhelming, and Maule summed up for a conviction. At the conclusion of this, counsel for the prisoner jumped up and said:

"I crave your lordship's pardon, but you have not referred to the prisoner's good character as proved by a number of witnesses."

"You are right, sir," said his lordship; and then, addressing the jury, he continued: "Gentlemen, I am requested to draw your attention to the prisoner's character, which has been spoken to by gentlemen I doubt not of the greatest respectability and veracity. If you believe them and also the witnesses for the prosecution it appears to me that they have established what to many persons may be incredible—namely, that even a man of piety and virtue occupying the position of Bible reader and Sunday-school teacher may be guilty of committing a heinous and grossly immoral crime."

To the defender of prisoners there is a mine of wisdom in the homely adage—"Let well alone."

Maule had always the ready word for any display of

conceit or impertinence. To an absurd liar who burst out in the witness-box, " My lord, you may believe me or not, but I have stated not a word that is false, for I have been wedded to truth from infancy."

" Very likely," replied the Judge, promptly and sternly, " but the question is how long you have been a widower."

The witness who will not speak up in the box and let everyone hear what he has to say is an abomination of desolation standing where he ought not. Maule, like every other judge, very properly loathed and detested him. " Witness ! " he called out to one of these offenders, " for the sake of God and your expenses, do speak out, man ! " And to another mumbler he spoke in warning tones : " Witness ! if you do not speak louder, I shall have to teach you the difference between *Aloud* and *Disallowed*."

Verbal puns and quips were not, however, Maule's speciality. I have heard it related of him that to a counsel who could not sound an *h*, and who referred constantly to an official as an " 'igh bailiff," Maule put the following question : " This official is quite unknown to me. I have never heard of an eye bailiff. I have heard of a bum bailiff. What is it you mean ? " I do not vouch for the truth of this story, which is also told of Baron Alderson and others.

Mock ceremony and exaggerated politeness in absurd circumstances seemed to give him vast pleasure. At Derby, once, when Maule was sentencing a prisoner, the governor of the gaol happened to pass between the prisoner in the dock and the judge, in order to hand a calendar to counsel. Maule thereupon called on the governor to stand up, and solemnly rebuked him. "Surely, sir, you know that you ought never to pass between two gentlemen when one gentleman is addressing the other." When the governor had apologised the Judge gave the prisoner seven years.

One witty decision of his is still good law, and is, I believe, followed by officials of Assize Courts. One of a jury locked up to consider their verdict, sent out for a glass of water, and the officer inquired of the Judge whether the request might be granted. "Well, sir," said Maule, "you are sworn to keep the jury without meat, drink, or fire. Now, water is not fire; water is not meat; and I should certainly hold that water is not drink, so let the fellow have a glass."

Maule showed no great kindness to the pretensions of the clergy, who probably often irritated him by their conceit of manner. Still, the terrible story told by Mr. Justice Hawkins of his amusing himself at the expense of a cleric whilst a wretched prisoner was being tried for his life is wholly inexcusable even if it has moments of delicious irony that make one almost forget its surroundings.

A man had murdered his wife. The vicar of his parish was called as to character. The defence was insanity, in which Maule did not greatly believe.

The vicar gave evidence that he had been a regular attendant at church until, without any apparent reason, he became a Sabbath-breaker, and after that the murder took place.

Maule then had a few words with the witness.

"You say you have been vicar of this parish for four-and-thirty years?"

"Yes, my lord."

"And during that time I daresay you have regularly performed the services of the Church."

"Yes, my lord."

"Did you have week-day services as well?"

"Every Tuesday, my lord."

"And did you preach your own sermons?"

"With an occasional homily of the Church."

"Your own sermon or discourse with an occasional homily. And was this poor man a regular attendant at all your services during the whole time you have been vicar?"

"Until he killed his wife, my lord."

"That follows. I mean up to the time of this Sabbath-breaking you spoke of. He regularly attended your ministrations and then killed his wife?"

"Exactly, my lord."

"Never missed the sermon, discourse, or homily of the Church, Sunday or week-day?"

"That is so, my lord."

"Did you write your own sermons, may I ask?"

"Oh yes, my lord."

Maule now made some calculations, and after a few words of mock courtesy to the parson read out the following results to Hawkins, who at the first thought all this interest in the vicar and his sermons looked well for the plea of insanity.

"This gentleman, Mr. Hawkins, has written with his own pen and preached or read with his own voice to this unhappy prisoner one hundred and four Sunday sermons or discourses, with an occasional homily every year. These, added to the week-day service, make exactly one hundred and fifty-six sermons, discourses, and homilies for the year. These, again, being continued for a space of time comprising, as the reverend gentleman tells us, no less than thirty-four years, gives us a grand total of five thousand three hundred and four sermons, discourses, or homilies during this unhappy man's life. Five thousand and three hundred and four," he repeated, gazing sternly at the vicar, " by the same person, however respectable and beloved as a pastor he might be, was what few of us could have gone through unless we were endowed with as much strength of mind as power of endurance.

" I was going to ask you, sir, did the idea ever strike you, when you talked of this unhappy being suddenly leaving your ministration, and becoming a Sabbath-breaker, that after thirty-four years he might want a little change ? Would it not be reasonable to suppose that the man might think he had had enough of it ? "

" It might, my lord."

" And would not that in your judgment, instead of showing that he was insane, prove that he was a *very sensible man ?* "

In spite of all this witty fooling, Hawkins was successful in his plea with the jury.

It is curious how Maule's desire to score off clerics crops up in the strangest places. In the great case of Lady Hewley's charities, where a question arose as to whether " Godly preachers " included clergymen of the

Church of England, Maule gave a very learned judicial opinion against their claim in the following words: "It is true, clergymen of the Church of England may and do preach the Gospel, but that is not their sole or most distinguishing function; and when 'preachers of the Gospel' are spoken of as a class, the clergy conforming to the Established Church are not, according to the ordinary use of language, comprehended."

No doubt this is sound in law and fact, but it might have been stated with greater regard for the feelings of the clergy.

One of the best-known Maule stories throws some light on his attitude towards current beliefs.

A little girl was in the witness-box, and, as is usual, before she was allowed to be sworn, she was examined by the Judge as to her understanding the nature of an oath, and her belief in a future state.

"Do you know what an oath is, my child?" said Maule.

"Yes, sir; I am obliged to tell the truth."

"And, if you do always tell the truth, where will you go to when you die?"

"Up to heaven, sir."

"And what will become of you if you tell lies?"

"I shall go down to the naughty place, sir."

"Are you quite sure of that?"

"Yes, sir, quite sure."

"Let her be sworn," said Maule. "It is quite clear she knows a great deal more than I do."

It seems a pity we have so few of Maule's recorded good sayings before he went to the Bench. He seems to have had a huge contempt for the generation of judges before whom he practised. When Mr. Justice Taunton rudely and irritatedly told him he was arguing like a child, he replied very sweetly: "I am well contented to be likened to a child, for a child if spared becomes in process of time a man; but once a bear, my lord, always a brute."

His famous saying to Bayley on the Midland Circuit has always been regarded by the junior Bar as an authoritative decision in favour of malt liquor. Bayley was drinking claret, when Maule reproved him, shouting out to him, "Claret be damned! Why don't you drink common porter and bring your understanding down to a level with the judges?"

Many Maule stories are not recorded at all, but only handed down to us by the oral traditions that still linger over the circuit wine on a winter night when two or three are gathered together and try to recall the glorious memories of forgotten days. Of such is the tale of the threatening letters. The case was one of great local interest, and on the morning of the second day the learned serjeant on one side made grave complaint that he and his client had received disgusting threatening letters. Up jumped the learned serjeant on the other side with a similar complaint.

"Brothers," said Maule, blandly holding up his hand for silence. "Brothers, I too have received threatening letters concerning this case, of a very abominable character; but it would ill befit me sitting on this Bench to say what I did with those letters sitting in another place."

When one has read and recalled all the witty ironies

and clever mockage of this strange character one is bound to admit that as far as records tell he was probably the greatest wit on the English Bench. Also it is fair to his memory to say that he did not make the numberless puny idle jests that some judicial humorists have been guilty of, and he tempered his humour with wisdom. In at least one case, the address to Hall the bigamist, his irony worked great public service ; but even this does not convince one that irony and wit are, properly speaking, judicial qualities. One reason why a judicial humorist is in danger of disaster is that, whatever the quality of his gift, it is bound by the altitude of his position to be received with a louder approbation than it deserves by its compulsory audience. *Non aliter* of schoolmasters. This in general is detrimental to its quality and aggravating to its quantity. One good word at least may be said about Maule, that he had a real rich gift of irony and always gave his hearers the best that was in him. There is no evidence that he ever played to the gallery. The reasons for and against admiration of his gift of irony are probably summed up in the phrase that he " couldn't help it." That is the only real excuse for irony.

Chapter IX : *Concerning Legal Reform*

NEARLY a hundred years ago, namely, in 1828, Lord Brougham came down to the House of Commons with a hatful of oranges and, aided by this refreshing fruit, spoke for six hours and three minutes by the clock on the defects in the laws of the realm and the measures necessary for removing the same. To any citizen interested in the social evolution of his country the speech is well worth reading again to-day. It did not deal with our penal statutes, " the most bloody and inefficient in the world," nor did it endeavour to probe " the bottomless pit of Chancery," but it was a scathing exposure of the abuses and anachronisms of our Common Law Courts, " featuring," as an American would say, not only many puerile fictions, much barbarism of procedure, and the quaint mummery of surviving customs, but also the daily misery and injustice that these things produced.

In a peroration of the noblest eloquence which remains the last best word ever spoken on legal reform Lord Brougham reminded his hearers of the boast of Augustus, who found a Rome of brick and left it of marble. " But," he continued, " how much nobler will be the sovereign's boast when he shall have it to say that he found law dear and left it cheap ; found it a sealed book, left it a living letter ; found it the patrimony of the rich, left it the inheritance of the poor; found it the two-edged sword of craft and oppression, left it the staff of honesty and the shield of innocence."

It is a fascinating task to anyone interested in legal history to go over the battlefields on which the various abuses he describes were attacked and destroyed, but the more practical business to-day is to inquire what remains to be done so that when the centenary of Lord Brougham's speech arrives we may be appreciably nearer the grand ideal he set before us.

It is always a matter of deep regret to me that when a layman writes about legal reform he lays the whole blame for the unsatisfactory condition of things on the shoulders of the lawyer and hints that in the main it is due to his selfishness and greed. There is sufficient precedent for reviling the individual instead of the system. Biblical references to lawyers are disconcerting; Rabelais has some unpleasant things to say about the Furred Law-cats; Bunyan has Mr. Legality with the mountain standing by his house—was it a mountain of costs?—Swift is cruel in his satire on judges and advocates; and Dickens has left us uncomfortable pictures of our law courts and their practitioners.

On the other hand, we may remember with pride that ever since the days of Marcus Tullius Cicero there has been a very general agreement among men that an education in law is perhaps the soundest preparation for political life, and we must recognise that modern citizens throughout the world, especially in English-speaking countries, very sensibly choose lawyers to represent them and place them in the highest positions of the State. The implicit confidence that business men have in their lawyers is a practical reply to satirical critics, and the fact that the advice and assistance of lawyers is readily sought in all the complications of social, trade, and domestic affairs is the real measure of the lawyers' service to their fellow-citizens.

The reason that lawyers are blamed for the defects of the legal system lies, I think, in the fact that lawyers constitute one of the oldest and most conservative trade unions in the world, and when they approach reform as a body they consider only the effect of it on shop rules and customs that have served in the past to affect favourably the rates of wages and the continuity of employment of their members. It is the way of all trade unions, and any individual who tries to look at reforms in his trade from any other than a union standpoint has always been suspect. It is said that a combination of attorneys on the Northern Circuit threatened Lord Brougham with a professional boycott if he went on with his schemes of legal reform, but time has given him the verdict and there is no lawyer of to-day who would uphold the abuses he attacked. For my part the great value of a trade union is the encouragement and assistance it gives to its younger members, the good-fellowship that exists in its ranks, and the standard of honesty and proficiency in their work that it demands from all who join it. In these things the Bar has a longer and more continuous record than any other trade union I know of, and it is still to-day, as it was in the time of Hampden and Harry Vane, a sound school of honesty, judgment, eloquence, and fellowship.

Concerning Legal Reform

I set this much down that I may not be misunderstood in writing freely of the present condition of our legal system. Like Mr. Crummles's pony, I have been "on circuit" from my earliest childhood, and I have the liveliest affection for all that pertains to the practice of the law. Such is my deep veneration for all that is good in our judicial system, and my respect for those in whose hands the administration of it is placed, that in writing at all about legal reform it is necessary to clearly dissociate myself from those who seek to lay all the blame for the shortcomings of our law at the gates of the Temple.

That there is room for a better economy in legal affairs is a commonplace. The necessity of the co-ordination and consolidation of legal matters has long been apparent to men of business and to those lawyers who can approach the subject from the citizen's point of view. What is wanted is more or less manifest. How to bring it about in spite of the apathy and opposition of a powerful profession deeply attached to its vested interests is not so clear. We may, however, believe that lawyers are eager for the welfare of the people, though we may decry their methods. Like the wife of the business man in the play, they "mean well but have no grasp." Remember, for instance, the historical account of the early efforts of Moses to establish Courts of Law. We read in the eighteenth chapter of Exodus that "Moses sat to judge the people: and the people stood by Moses from morning unto the evening." Then Moses' father-in-law Jethro arrived and inquired what he was attempting to do, and asked Moses: "Why sittest thou thyself alone, and all the people stand by thee from morning unto evening ?" Moses explained that it was his idea of instituting a law court, and his father-in-law replied : " The thing thou doest is not good." Then Jethro set forth his idea of legal reform, and it remains as clear a statement of the true principle of the construction of law courts as one could wish for to-day. He " chose able men out of all Israel and made them heads over the people, rulers of thousands, rulers of hundreds, rulers of fifties, and rulers of tens. And they judged the people at all seasons : the hard causes they brought unto Moses, but every small matter they judged themselves." Jethro, the man of business ideas, came to the rescue of Moses, the Law-giver, and Moses had the wisdom to accept his advice. Until that happens in this country we shall never have anything but an unworkmanlike, uneconomical legal system clogging the wheels of business and weighing heavily on the poorer members of the community.

Many think that legal reform is of necessity a lawyer's business and that a layman cannot understand, much less solve, the problems of it. That is wholly an error. For the last hundred years questions of legal reform have been thrashed out and discussed and illustrated in the pamphlets and papers of legal writers, the Reports of Commissions, and the publication of statistics. These can be read and digested by any ordinary citizen. Some of them —as the Divorce Commission—have been the outcome of public discontent with existing laws. From time to time we find small reforms forced by the general body of citizens on the lawyers, for hitherto such work has always been done in the teeth of professional opposition. It would be interesting to dwell on the pagan mysteries of special pleading and the religious enthusiasm with which lawyers fought in its defence. In 1847 John George Phillimore, the jurist, wrote with magnificent scorn of the folly and iniquity of "special demurrers." "The man who would waste a moment in arguing with the advocates of special demurrers is unworthy of all leisure." He expressed the view that these "absurdities" would speedily be abolished, but it was not until the Common Law Procedure Act of 1852 that they disappeared, and many other similar absurdities, such as the indictment, have lingered on into our own generation. Phillimore was certainly right when he said that arguing with lawyers about the absurdities of the law is waste of time. Any layman of reasonable education can read for himself the returns and reports of the various State departments dealing with law. In these he will find not only the facts and figures necessary to form conclusions, but the reasoned opinions of all the great thinkers both jurists and practical men on what is wanted in our legal system to make it useful to the community and also such arguments as the obscurantists can bring forward against any and every proposed change.

But it is scarcely to be expected that in the literary affections of the man in the street the Blue Book will ever take the place of the Yellow Press. And until some genius arises capable of making legal affairs in print comprehensible as well as entertaining it is doubtful whether we shall reach that force of popular push which alone nowadays compels politicians to toe the line of social reform. Still, things are looking brighter for legal reform than they have ever looked since the days of Lord Brougham. The splendid series of articles to " The Times " by Lord Birkenhead are certainly the most inspiring words that have been uttered to the public by a great legal authority since the speeches that Lord Brougham delivered in 1828. But a Lord Chancellor has perforce to deal with questions of Land Transfer, Divorce, Salaries, Fees, and Judicial Organisation, not so much from the point of view of the common citizen, but with an eye to political possibilities and the big interests of commerce and business. It is of legal reform in the narrower sense of adapting legal organisation to the wants of our poorer citizens, and in these matters alone, that my smaller but continuous experience enables me to speak with some authority.

Although citizens to-day are naturally suspicious of new Ministries, I am not clear that a Minister of Law is not a condition precedent to any real reform. Perhaps the way out of it most consonant to English methods would be to relieve the Lord Chancellor of most of his judicial and political duties and, granting him an adequate staff, allow him to gradually assume such ministerial powers as he thought advisable for the purpose of carrying out reforms.

I do not think the ordinary citizen recognises how slender is the actual ministerial control upon judicial affairs. It is, of course, essential to English justice that the judge in his judicial capacity should be entirely unhampered by departmental interference. But this might surely be attained under the business direction of a Minister of Law who had under his control all the methods of organisation and order in legal affairs. For as matters stand at present there is little or no co-ordination among the different Courts. Jurisdictions overlap. Some great commercial communities have insufficient legal service, and some small, old-world citizens are burderned by uneconomic visits of legal bigwigs.

The High Court Judges, for instance, are in a great measure as regards the arrangement of business a law unto themselves. They meet and settle when and where they should sit, what circuits they propose to attend, and what Courts they should form for the business at hand. However desirous it might be for a branch of the High Court to be set up in any large city in England and there to hold continuous sittings, giving the provincial the same legal service as the Londoner, we have no existing minister who could ordain such a thing.

The County Courts are under the jurisdiction of the Lord Chancellor and also of the Treasury, which has a special department devoted to them ; the Courts of the Justices of the Peace are under the control of the Home Office ; whilst the actual Courts themselves and the official buildings belong to the Office of Works, and much equipment is provided by the Stationery Office. Bankruptcy affairs are in the hands of the Board of Trade, and the Chancellor of the Duchy of Lancaster exercises local legal control.

The various Courts, no doubt, arrange their business to the best of their ability, to serve the public, but there is no one dominating mind with power to make the most economic use of all their services for the benefit of the community. Fifty years ago Lord Bramwell urged that a better consolidation and co-ordination of all our Courts was necessary to the public service. His view was that County Courts, or similar district inferior Courts of first instance, should be made constituent branches of the High Court of Justice, and that every civil proceeding should commence in the County Court and be tried there unless the defendant chose to remove it to the High Court. To the lawyers of his own day this was a revolutionary proposal, and in later years when it was again suggested it was considered inimical to the interests of the Bar, to which Lord Bramwell replied: "If there is any disparagement or injury to the Bar for the benefit of the public the Bar must undergo it; that is all."

Meanwhile, in spite of the absence of a Minister of Law to direct matters, and in the face of much legal opposition and some disinterested and clear-sighted legal assistance, the trend of events and the working of the law of the survival of the suitable has contrived to give a jurisdiction to the County Courts which has made them outside a few big centres the Common Law Courts of the country. In 1830 Lord Brougham proposed "local District Courts" with a jurisdiction of £100 in contract, £50 in tort and an unlimited jurisdiction by consent. The suggestion fairly took the breath of the profession away and of course came to nothing. It was not until 1847 that County Courts were established, and then only with a jurisdiction of £20. Up to that time the Assizes did all the common law work of the country, but from 1847 there have been two competing and overlapping systems, and the natural result has been that the cheaper and more accessible system has been the most popular, and little by little has acquired greater power until in 1903 it attained the jurisdiction of £100 which Lord Brougham had proposed for it in 1830.

To understand the present working conditions of the common law courts in the country to-day let us make a short legal survey of things as they are in my own county of Kent. The county has an area of 971,991 acres and contains a population of 1,045,591. Prior to the establishment of County Courts all its common law affairs were carried on by the King's Bench Division, and every case arising within its borders had to be tried at its somewhat inaccessible capital of Maidstone. In the days of my childhood, when local venue obtained, the Assizes at places like Maidstone and Guildford lasted for many days or even weeks, and my father, Serjeant Parry, used often to take a house at these places, so that my earliest recollections of the law are faint memories of such great figures as Bovill, Ballantine, Hawkins, and Shee, who found ample scope for their energies and abilities in the cause list of the Home Circuit.

This came to an end in 1875 with the abolition of local venue, and as soon as the men of Kent were allowed to set down cases where they wished, the convenience of London and the inconvenience of Maidstone for the populous western portion of the county led to litigants setting down their causes for trial in London. At the same time the County Court jurisdiction was being bit by bit continuously enlarged so that very little work was left for Maidstone Assizes except the libels, slanders, and breach of promise actions which for some mysterious reason are considered too intricate and important for trial by any lower tribunal than the High Court.

There is still in Maidstone an existing Court of Pleas with a wide jurisdiction, but it has not done any work since 1778. There is also, it is said, a Court of Pie Poudre, a Court of Conservancy, and a Court Leet, but they are all archæological shadows.

Two Assizes are still held at Maidstone for civil work, and we find that in 1913—and I use these figures as they give the last year of normal work—there were twenty-three actions entered for trial, fifteen of which were tried and £1285 recovered. This was eight days' work and is considerably in excess of the usual amount of time spent at Maidstone. What these cases were and how far it was necessary that they should be tried by a High Court Judge does not appear.

The issue of High Court Writs and all the interlocutory proceedings in High Court actions are carried out in what are known as District Registries ; Kent has four of these Registries, and the following table shows their activities at a glance :—

District Registry.	No. of Proceedings.	Amount Recovered.
Maidstone . .	42	£1261
Dover . . .	16	£ 563
Ramsgate . .	65	£1226
Rochester . .	23	£ 652
	146	£3702

In each town I have mentioned it appears that the District Registrar of the High Court is at the same time the Registrar of the County Court, and he sits and conducts his business in the same office and with the same clerks. If for the saving of space one may be allowed to use the military notation, one may say that as D.R.H.C. he does the same work as R.C.C., but he commences the action with a writ instead of a plaint. He is a veritable Pooh Bah. No doubt as a High Court official he has a proper contempt for himself as a County Court official, but at the same time the more important work and better remuneration that he receives as a County Court official enables him to hold up his head in his own presence, so to speak, and offer the retort courteous to any patronising airs that his High Court self may try to put on in what, after all, are the offices of the County Court.

The work done by this official is, therefore, not work done in any real sense in the High Court. No pretence can be made that this class of work requires any better or different grade of human official to that which does County Court work. It is a pure example of overlapping jurisdiction, of the same class of work being done by one and the same official in different ways with different names for the same things, and under parallel procedures. It is true that as you issue a writ in the High Court, or an ordinary plaint or a default summons in the County Court, so you proceed in one Court or the other, and sometimes in both, to recover your debt; but these openings are like the gambits at chess, different ways of beginning the same game, and ought to be playable on the same board and with the same set of men and under the same rules.

Assuming, however, that we set down this £3702 as

money recovered by the High Court, which technically it is, we have in 1913 a total of £4987 collected, by means of the Assizes at Maidstone and the four District Registries, by the King's Bench Division. Let us now turn to the work of the County Court. Kent has two County Court Circuits, the eastern district taking up the whole time of one judge, the western sharing a judge with the metropolitan district of Lambeth. It may be said that the county finds employment for a judge and a half. These judges preside over twenty-eight Courts, and each Court has a Registrar. The judgments recovered in these Courts in 1913 amounted to £37,024. Even if the High Court is rightly credited with the amount recovered in District Registries it seems clear, as far as money can speak, that the common law business in Kent has found its own way into the County Courts and left the King's Bench Division.

Suppose, then, that the County Court were a branch of the High Court or that a minister had control of the whole system, what would be his first step on discovering this state of affairs? He would, I think, make up his mind to have one Registry and one Registrar who would issue only one kind of process; whether he chose to call it a writ or a plaint or a summons would be no matter, but he would certainly make a rule that all common law proceedings started in the same office with a document of the same type and hue. This in itself would mean a far-reaching reform, because it could only be done by making County Courts branches of the main legal system instead of legal local side-shows as they are to-day, and it would mean scrapping existing practices and procedure and by their consolidation and fusion making one system of proceeding common to all actions.

In Kent, as I have shown, this happens geographically and humanly speaking to-day. A Kentish man goes into the same office and sees the same official whenever he wants to start an action at law, but he has the choice of two different overlapping systems, either of which, with certain and uncertain risks as to costs, he can adopt, and the two procedures only vary in points of detail.

It would seem from the figures I have quoted that, assuming every action in Kent were begun by the issue of a plaint in the County Court, the great bulk of the cases heard would remain there as of course. Indeed all the cases now tried in the so-called District Registries would continue in the same office, and the only outstanding matters to consider would be the few cases which are tried every year at Maidstone Assizes.

It must be remembered that the law at present does not permit libel, slander, and breach of promise to be tried as of right in County Courts, and therefore at present these cases, however unimportant and trumpery, are bound to waste much of the Judge's time at Assizes. When, however, all actions are begun in the County Court, litigants will only seek to remove them for some good cause and should only be allowed to do so for some very substantial reason. The case once started, the Registrar will have full power to direct the manner of its trial. If on the application of either plaintiff or defendant he comes to the conclusion that the matter is one really worthy of trial by a High Court Judge, he will direct it so to be tried, and then the parties can take it to London if they wish, just as they do to-day, or if it is of an exceptional nature a High Court Judge will come into Kent specially to try it. In a word, the Registrar will be an organiser and sifter of the work to be done, allotting each case to its proper Court for trial and never allowing the time of the High Court to be wasted on matters that can be satisfactorily settled in the County Court.

I cannot honestly commend the County Court as a cheap entertainment for poor litigants, yet as compared with the High Court both for cost and speed it is much less exhausting to purse and temper. Figures and statistics are dull things and I refrain from them wherever it is possible, but the bills of costs cited below give such a graphic picture of the amenities of the two Courts that I need scarcely apologise for their introduction.

Before the Divorce Commission, Mr. Dendy, the District Registrar of the High Court and Registrar of the County Court at Newcastle-on-Tyne, handed in some interesting tables of actual costs. He had taxed the bills in seventy-seven Assize actions in the Newcastle District Registry. The average amount of costs in these was £108 5s. 10d. Since 1903, when the jurisdiction of the County Court was raised from £50 to £100, he had taxed the costs in forty-seven actions tried under the extended jurisdiction. The average costs was £30 as against the £108 in the High Court. He emphasised the value of the figures by saying: "I would like to point out the curious result that not only is the average just under one-third, but the highest is just one-third and the lowest is just one-third—the highest was £106 as against £326, and the lowest was £8 14s. 6d. as against £36 9s. 8d.—and therefore I think you may say from my experience in that particular district the cost of an extended jurisdiction action in the County Court is just one-third of an Assize action."

Every unnecessary Assize action, therefore, mulcts the loser in treble the costs he would have to pay in the County Court, and this is not only a serious waste, but a terrible penalty upon poor or middle-class litigants who are victims of the system.

Of course, in order to carry out any real co-ordination of the Courts and to make all the Courts open to all members of the Bar great inroads will have to be made upon the old Circuit system. No one has a deeper or more affectionate remembrance of circuit days than I have, but I have no fear at all that whatever reforms are necessary they will eradicate that spirit of fellowship which the circuits fostered and which animates all honest members of the English Bar.

Nor should it be thought that a reformer is necessarily a traitor to Circuit traditions. There have always been good circuiteers who recognised that the needs of the community and the vested interests of the circuits did not coincide and that new methods were necessary. Sixty years ago there existed an admirable society of earnest and learned men known as the Juridical Society, and you may find many excellent essays on the matters now under discussion in the transactions of that body, printed in two somewhat scarce volumes bearing date 1855 to 1863.

Bethell and Bramwell were their Presidents, and many men of note at the Bar were among their members.

Frederick Lawrence, the gifted biographer of Fielding, wrote an admirable paper on circuit reform in 1863. The problem as he stated it is still our problem :

" The England of to-day," he writes, " it is obvious at the outset, differs very widely indeed from the England for which our present circuit system was devised and for which it continued for a long period well adapted. It would be marvellous indeed if a plan which satisfied the necessities of more primitive times—which sufficed for the days of the Plantagenets, the Tudors, and the Stuarts —should work equally well in a widely different and more complex state of society. Not only have we to provide for a densely populated commercial and manufacturing nation in place of a thinly populated agricultural country, but improved methods of locomotion now render results attainable which, however desirable, must have appeared impracticable to the early lawyer and legislator."

If this was true in 1863, how much more true it is in 1922! Lawrence points out that to harass important judges with useless journeys and employ them upon inferior duties is bad economy. He instances no less than twenty-two Assize towns having less than 10,000 inhabitants, and complains that they are ill adapted to afford accommodation for witnesses, jurors, attorneys, and counsel, and that they are situated out of the most direct routes. He, too, was impressed by the fact that the costs in many cases were out of all proportion to the importance of the matter in dispute between the parties. His proposal of reform is the one that has held the field since and will continue to do so until the reform is made: " Instead of visiting fifty-four places twice a year the

Judges might with less labour transact all the civil and criminal business of the circuits by sitting in ten or twelve of our largest towns—the centres of populous districts and accessible by the most direct lines of railway —three times every year." If that was a business proposal in 1863, how much more is it a business proposal in 1922. He then proceeds to discuss the position of the Bar. In a pleasant passage he reminds his brethren of the evolution of circuits:

"When the Circuit Bar rode through the country with the Judges, the stately cavalcade was doubtless much admired as it resolutely faced the winds of March, or swept over the green sward in summer time beneath the shade of English oaks. Yet when in process of time highway roads improved and ceased to be impassable half the year, barristers took advantage of them like other people for greater ease and facility of locomotion, though they still endeavoured to preserve their exclusive character by avoiding public vehicles and by travelling in private carriages and post chaises. When the rail began to supersede the road another revolution was at hand. Very timidly at first but from sheer necessity the Circuit Bars trusted themselves to *public* conveyances."

This last touch is a quaint but forcible picture of the attitude of the Bar towards all new things. Nowadays, with large local Bars at Manchester, Liverpool, Birmingham, and many other centres, the Circuit system has lost most of its usefulness. When central legal districts are formed the Courts will be as open to the Bar of England as the High Courts of London and the County Courts of all the country. The necessity of a tied house system for legal advice and advocacy was necessary to attract lawyers to out-of-the-way places when travelling was expensive and hazardous. To-day it is as out of date as turnpikes and highwaymen, and as a matter of fact barristers do not "go circuit" in the old sense at all, but go to such places as they have briefs or the expectation thereof. The old circuit days, when a young man travelled religiously round the circuit twice a year and was one of a hundred at Grand Court singing the old chorus—

> "All round the Circuit I goes without a guinea,
> All round the Circuit for two months and a day,
> And if anybody axes me the reason why I do it
> It's because I don't know how to earn it any other way."

—those days are as dead and gone as the merry drunken times at Lancaster when Eldon and his friends delivered a bogus brief to Boswell whom they had picked up in the street over night, and the little man solemnly moved for a writ of *quare adhaesit pavimento* before the judge, who enjoyed the jest as much as the members of the Bar.

Assuming, therefore, that there existed a Minister of Law with power to co-ordinate and arrange the business of the Courts of the country in the interests solely of the community and without interference from vested interests, the first task before him would, I think, be to provide the same legal facilities for the trial of actions in the North and West and Midlands that already exist in London and the South. He would, I think, in looking at the statistics find that there was a large centre of legal business at Manchester and Liverpool, at Birmingham, at Leeds, at Cardiff and Swansea, and at Bristol. These are all natural centres of litigation for their different districts, and in each of these centres he would seek to give the inhabitants similar legal services of the High Court to those that are obtainable in London. The High Court Judges should be relieved from visiting the smaller towns as they do now, but they should give such continuous service in the great centres as is required to put the North and the West and the Midlands on an equality with the South. In 1877, John Day, Q.C., afterwards the well-known judge, urged that Circuit Judges should only sit " at certain great centres, such as Newcastle, Liverpool, Manchester, York, Birmingham, Peterborough, Bristol, Swansea, and Exeter."

The idea, therefore, is no new one, and the new District Registries that I propose would sift and arrange the work, but would look to their local High Court centre for High Court work and would not request the judge's services away from the centre unless, as before suggested, for the trial of some action of peculiar importance. It would be found, I think, that five geographical centres were all that were needed and that if two judges were available for these, as and when required, and their time never wasted on trivial and unimportant matters, it would be far more satisfactory to business men than the present state of affairs.

I lay stress on the necessity of two judges for the following reason. In each of these centres it should be a part of the duty of the two High Court Judges to sit as a Divisional Court and hear appeals from the District

Courts and from all magisterial courts. In 1913, taking ten consecutive County Courts in the north of England, there were seventeen appeals, and taking ten consecutive courts in London and the neighbourhood there were fifty-one. Now, this rate of three to one does not denote that the cases were better tried or more complicated in one district than another; it merely means that a southerner has an Appeal Court at his door and a northerner has not. Whilst multiplicity of appeals is bad for the community, reasonable access to appeal is good for everybody, and especially for the judge presiding over a District Court whose work of necessity has to be done without the legal assistance and the library munitions that are at hand in every legal centre. Work without criticism is apt to degenerate, and, however watchful and careful a judge may be, he will never be the less so for knowing that his decisions are open to a cheap and speedy appeal.

With a Law Ministry and the co-ordination of all Courts, civil and criminal, it would be possible to consider seriously many other questions of legal reform. Perhaps it would be found well to have District Judges of more than one grade, and it might become the practice to advance them to more responsible posts. A Dean may become an Archbishop, but until the reign of the present Lord Chancellor a County Court Judge or a Stipendiary Magistrate always remained in the position to which he was appointed unless he accepted an offer to go into other Government service.

Any consolidation of County Courts with the High Court will make it necessary to reorganise the staff of the

County Courts. Registrars at present are allowed to remain in private practice—indeed, it is necessary they should do so, as their remuneration would otherwise be insufficient for their support. They are to a great extent paid by fees, an arrangement which savours of an Elizabethan age. As far back as 1878 a Commission recognised that it would not be right to entrust a Registrar with judicial functions as long as he is permitted to practise in his district, and until a Registrar can try cases of small amount the Jethro principle of devolution cannot be carried out, and the judge must continue to travel to small places to find little or nothing to do.

A Registrar who is a permanent Civil servant could transact all the small cases in a group of Courts and do all the registry work for District and High Courts and send on the larger cases to their appointed destination. It has been long recognised that this ought to be done. In London the High Court officials are all public servants, and the larger urban County Courts to-day have permanent Registrars. The chief clerks, too, of all Courts should be graded Civil servants, as they are in the High Court in London to-day. The duties in London and the country are the same, and there can be no sound reason why the pay and the status should be altogether different.

The Irish County Courts have a permanent travelling Registrar, but in England the best course would be to have one Registrar for a group of districts who should be a Civil servant. If at the same time he was to act as clerk to the magistrates, there would be enough work to justify a reasonable salary. A Law Ministry could consider how far the present administration of the criminal law by means of unpaid magistrates at Petty and Quarter Sessions and Recorders of varying experience in large and small boroughs is an economical and satisfactory arrangement, and whether it would not be better to make local central criminal districts presided over by the District Judges. In Ireland the County Court Judges have criminal jurisdiction, and there seems no reason why similar judges should not be available here for this class of work.

Once the District Courts of the kingdom were co-ordinated with the High Court there could be no excuse for preventing poor people from having access to those Courts in matters of divorce. The general question of Divorce Reform is a matter of social urgency, but in the present age to give facilities for divorce to the rich and to withhold similar facilities from the poor is inexcusable. All local divorce cases might be tried in County Courts unless the parties for some good cause removed a particular case to the High Court.

At present all divorce cases are tried in London, although an experiment is to be made of their trial at some central Assize towns. This, as I have already shown, will not cut down the legal expenses, and though it will mitigate some of the cost of travelling and entertaining witnesses it will still leave a very heavy burden to be borne by the poor.

Sir George Lewis was no sentimentalist; he had the largest business knowledge of the working of divorce laws of any solicitor in England, and had been in practice since the passing of the Divorce Act in 1857. His view, therefore, of the effect of the present state of things on the lives of poorer citizens may be accepted as authoritative, and the fact that it was confirmed by practically all the witnesses who approached the subject undisturbed by ecclesiastical bias and was in effect accepted by the Commission renders it the final word on the subject.

" Now, with regard to the poor ? " he is asked, and he replies with emphasis :

" Oh, it is a shocking position is the law of divorce for them. There is no divorce for them. As the law now stands there is no divorce. Unless there is an alteration in the law it will continue as it has always existed."

" Will you tell us why you say that ? "

" Because the poor have not the means to come to the Divorce Court in London, and if they want divorce they must come to London for it."

He is then asked if he had any alternative suggestion to make as to constituting a tribunal to deal with divorce in the country, and replied that he certainly had. " I think it is an insult," he said, " to tell the County Court Judges they are not competent to try questions of fact, whether adultery has been committed, or whether cruelty has been committed." He referred to the Summary Jurisdiction Act of 1895, which gave lay magistrates power to try these questions in relation to separation and maintenance orders, and continued :

" So that Parliament has already given to these gentlemen who are not lawyers, who have no experience in legal matters, the right to order judicial separations amongst the poor, and to give them the right to determine whether a woman has committed adultery or not. I say in face of that for anyone to come here and to argue that the County Court Judges should not be entrusted with these duties is to me astonishing. But I wish further to point out under this Act that if the husband commits adultery, the wife has no protection whatsoever. The justices have no power to inquire into it. The husband may commit adultery, and what is the poor wife to do? He may continue to commit adultery, and then, in disgust and horror at the position in which she is placed, she may say, 'I will go away,' and she goes away. The Court has no power to give her alimony; she cannot take her children away with her; there is no power of the Court to order that she shall be allowed to take them. When she is pining for her children after a time all she can do is to go to the Chancery Division of the High Court and under the Infant Custody Act to ask for her children to be given her. Of course, it is impossible for her to do that, as she has not the means to do anything of the sort. So it seems to me the law, as far as the poor are concerned, is in a painful and disgraceful condition."

And so it is likely to remain until there exists a business department charged with the duty of carrying out the reforms that have been considered and reported upon by the Divorce Commission. It may be thought that if these legal reforms were really pressing there would be an almost unanimous demand for them from lawyers themselves, but the history of legal reform goes to show that until the general body of citizens began to take interest in these matters a lawyer who preached reforms has always been a voice crying in the wilderness.

The Bar and the Law Society, speaking as trade unions

on behalf of their members, seldom manage to impress the public mind with the idea that they are capable of taking broad public views of the administration of the law as a social service, but rather seem to take pleasure in holding out the professions as institutions made for the sustenance and enrichment of their members. They regard Law Ministers, Land Registries, Abolition of Assizes, establishment of District Courts, local divorce, and any proposed reforms that are brought before them merely from the point of view of existing shop rules.

The lawyer trade unionist is a short-witted die-hard. All change is distasteful to him. Nothing could have been more unfortunate than the discussions of the Bar and the Law Society on the eve of the introduction of women into the professions. Much of the work of a lawyer, and especially of a solicitor, is peculiarly adapted to women, and after the success of women in the more difficult field of medicine one might have hoped that the leading trade unionists among the lawyers would have had sufficient sense to remember the mistakes and defeat of the doctors and not to have led their members into an undignified contest with only one possible end to it. The matter being a public question and the public considering it an urgent one, the die-hards were swept into obscurity and the reform was made.

And in course of time these reforms which I have outlined will seize the imagination and interest of the public, and those of them that are sound and necessary will be brought about. Greatly as I esteem the members of both branches of the profession in their individual capacity, I have very little use for their collective verdicts on social subjects. On these matters I look to the example of lawyers like Lord Brougham and Lord Bramwell and Lord Birkenhead, who have been clear-sighted enough to realize the evils of the systems by which they were immediately surrounded and have had sufficient of the poet in them to see clear visions of a better future. They have been always " ready and willing "—to use the cant phrase of the pleader—to inquire into existing defects of the Law and to propose measures of reform. True to their trade union in all matters of fellowship and domestic discipline, they have regarded the profession of the Law as a sacred trust in which the lawyer has a public duty forbidding him to consider matters of personal welfare when the wider interests of fellow-citizens are at stake.

Chapter X: *Concerning the Future of Portia*

MY Dear Portia,

It is flattering of you—and flattery has its uses at the Bar before some tribunals—it is flattering, I say, that you should ask an old Dogberry like myself, who has probably listened to more unskilful advocacy than anyone living, for some practical hints on your future prospects. You tell me that you want to become a legal "best seller," and I do not see why you should not succeed in your ambitions. Someone does, and it is always cheering to remember that the "best seller" is not necessarily the highest form of literature.

Your intention of going into Parliament and becoming a judge, though not a new one, is according to precedent, and in your chosen profession deference to precedent is considered a virtue. At the same time, a barrister who becomes a member of Parliament does not always attain to a judgeship, though the rate of exchange between a safe seat in Parliament and a seat on the bench of the High Court is often quoted in the lobby by political experts and allowed for in the odds by the bookmakers of the robing room.

But do not, I pray you, dabble too determinedly,

whilst you are a student, in the politics of the moment. It is scarce safe to attach oneself at an early age to any particular side or special patron. It does not look well in the public eye to chop and change your political principles too frequently, and it is impossible to foresee which side or which individual may have seisin of the demesne when in a few years you are ready to take the field.

I was glad to read in the papers that you had passed in Roman Law and that so many of your fair companions had gained honours in the examinations. Do not be disheartened by the somewhat unchivalrous reminder of a writer in the law papers that " examination successes do not justify the confident expectations that women will secure corresponding triumphs in the forensic arena." The unknown legal warriors who write in law journals must be suffered gladly. They know perhaps what it is to pass in Roman Law with confident expectation of forensic triumphs and to be non-suited in the battle of life.

And it is well that you should understand that, though examinations must be passed, yet when they are passed they are best forgotten. The Art of Advocacy in which your namesake made such a distinct hit has very little to do with a study of the Pandects. Success in advocacy depends mainly on character. The Domus rightly expects that you should be a person of sound learning and religious education, since, as the great D'Aguesseau said, the order of advocates is " as noble as virtue." But the average solicitor will look for the more worldly attributes of judgment, courage, wit, and eloquence: and for my part I have never believed that these qualities have any sex consciousness.

As you know, I was for a long time in a hopeless minority in advocating the opening of our profession to women. My brethren were resolutely opposed to your entrance among them. This discourteous attitude was not, my dear niece, personal to yourself. You will find that the dwellers in the Temple are very gallant gentlemen, but they are also fanatical trade unionists and as such objected to you and your young friends as dilutees. It is a horrible word, no doubt, but you will have to learn and listen to many such jargonical words in your new trade; nor must you fail to study carefully all the shop rules of the Bar which are called "etiquette," and these you will talk about reverently and pay such heed to as shall not clash with your personal advancement.

You will find that the union makes much play about a minimum wage both for its own members and those unskilled labourers known as barristers' clerks. There is, however, no rule about maximum fees, and the greater the figures on your brief the higher the honour in which you will be held by the outside world. One curious shop rule will no doubt please you at first. You will find that all the members of your union go on strike every summer for two months. It is a preferable habit, no doubt, to the more common one adopted by most unions of striking at odd seasons without notice, but it is said to cause some public inconvenience. And now you are yourself a member of the union you must never forget that the strict boycott of the dilutee must always be maintained, and even during the Great War the Bar consistently refused to permit dilutees to do even the unskilled work of consenting to judgment.

With these things in your mind you will not wonder, then, that many of your present colleagues were in the past very antagonistic to woman labour. But now that you have won the battle you need not fear but that you will be given all that Huxley and Mill and your best friends have ever asked for you—" a fair field and no favour." You will be freely allowed to enter for Parliament, the Woolsack, or any of the legal consolation stakes on the card. But you must remember you cannot be given a handicap. Every contest you enter for will be a real championship—not a ladies' championship. You will have to compete with your fellow-man under the same rules and drive off from the same tees.

When you are called to the Bar you will commence as advocate, no doubt, in the County Court, where you will find justice is administered quite as indifferently as it is in the High Court, except that there is more of it and the pace is quicker. It is like the difference between county cricket and village cricket. We have no three-day matches in the village court; everyone goes in for a short innings and a merry one, the game is brought to a conclusion in a reasonable time, and we play on after twilight to finish the match. The County Court of to-day is the advocate's kindergarten. And you will hear excellent advocacy there, though the bulk is not always equal to the sample. I look back over nearly thirty years and remember angelic advocates who are now High Court Judges, Attorney-Generals, even Lord Chancellors. I did not altogether entertain them unawares, and when their triumphs are told I can shake my old head and say, "I told you so." Yes, yes, Dogberry is "a fellow that hath had his losses," for the best boys in the kindergarten are moved up to higher things and a new generation comes along to sharpen their wits at the old grindstone.

Nevertheless, the County Courts are well served at the present, and it is pleasant to think that the day is not far off when the younger men will in their turn have climbed the heights of fame. Indeed, my dear Portia, I shall hope to see you often before me down at Lambeth. There are many cases where the affairs of women are discussed where your practical knowledge will be very valuable to the Bench. Nothing to me is more unworthy of the dignity of the Court than our present dealing with dress-making litigation. In Admiralty cases a judge is not expected to know how to hand reef and steer : he has the assistance of a nautical assessor, and where doctors disagree he may have a medical assessor. But in a dress-making affray, which is indeed a fierce and furious contest, he has to rush in between Madame Mantalini and Miss Montmorency and listen to shrill complaints about gussets, flounces, and basting, and pretend to understand what has happened when a dress piece has been "cut on the cross."

At times a judge may be asked to interview counsel and parties in camera and observe with his own eyes the want of coincidence between the garment and the figure, a very delicate and embarrassing position for a shy and retiring personality and one which would be pleasanter to all parties if Portia were there to chaperone Dogberry and explain to him what it was really all about.

I am sorry that you and your sister students permitted the Bench to decide what you should wear in Court. I do not myself fancy you in a wig and gown. Woman having decided to unite herself to a new profession, it is only seemly that she should have been allowed to design her wedding garment. Remember that, though your namesake was careful to ask old Bellario to send down to the common ferry that trades with Venice not only his notes about the case but his " garments," yet she never wears them. At least, none of the Portias I recalled ever appeared in the old gentleman's reach-me-downs, but wore very nice well-fitting and beautiful robes evidently designed by some skilful dressmaker.

And when you think of Portia let me warn you not to expect to repeat her success on every occasion that you appear in Court. *R. v. Shylock* was an exceptionally lucky get-out for Antonio and has, I believe, been overruled in America. The prosecution took place before the Venetian County Quarter Sessions with the old Duke in the Chair and the Clerk of the Peace away on vacation. That sly fox Bellario knew very well that the point of law he sent along to Portia was a bad one, and he was not going to injure his reputation by arguing it. You will find in your professional career that your learned leader is often called away to another Court when the case is hopeless, and the points assigned to you to argue in the Court of Appeal will not be the most fool-proof.

However, Portia showed good advocacy in doing her best to settle the case with the old Jew on fair terms of payment before she risked her client's case by arguing bad law before a weak tribunal.

I have seen Portias who distinctly ogled the Duke, and that I need hardly tell you is decidedly unprofessional. Never, my dear girl, be tempted, however desperate your client's fortunes may be, to try and influence the male members of the jury by the overt use of the glad eye. In former days it might have succeeded, but now I feel sure your sister jurors would resent such conduct and their disapproval would be expressed in their verdict. These, however, are matters of taste in which I am sure you will not err.

On all these legal matters I can speak to you with authority, since in these affairs no one will suspect my place, much less my years; but when you ask me for some hints concerning Parliamentary deportment I am not on such familiar ground. I have, however, consulted my old and venerated friend Turveydrop, M.P., admitted, by all who know him, to be the greatest expert on these matters. He inquired at once if you were the daughter or niece of a statesman in office. If you were, he assured me that you might safely adopt a modest demeanour and rely on your own undoubted merits to place you in some good office.

But in the absence of even an Under-Secretarial cousinship he advises that it will be necessary for you to think out some method not too hackneyed and suitable to your disposition to call the attention of overburdened ministers to your interesting personality. As to the actual means to pursue he was not very explicit, but he made, what was to me, a most interesting suggestion. Just as he was called away by the division bell he turned to me and was kind enough to say, " My dear

Dogberry, you are, as we all know, a man of literary attainments and have on several occasions written yourself down—you know what I mean—to the public level. Now, think over in your own mind the type of heroine in fiction that you as a man of the world, a taxpayer, and a party politician would vote for as a lady candidate."

Somehow as I strolled home across the Park I felt that if I could find the right solution to Turveydrop's problem I should place in your hands the key to Parliamentary success. The idea fascinated me. I took it seriously. I weighed in my memory the attributes of all the heroines I could remember from Moll Flanders to the Second Mrs. Tanqueray. I could not find one that would really shine in that strange conglomeration of sincerity, earnestness, clap-trap, and twaddle which form a chemical combination known in Westminster as the Parliamentary Atmosphere. Portia herself was more eloquent than convincing. Beatrice, too direct and witty. Rosalind, with Touchstone as an election agent, would never be taken seriously by the agricultural interests. Moreover, a Shakespearean heroine would, I felt sure, rush into the arms of some dashing young under-Secretary, sacrifice herself on the wrong altar, and her political career would evaporate in a shower of confetti.

Becky Sharp has of course the true political instinct and could lead every party with equal success, but then we do not want more leaders of this type and I was searching for a working back bench member, since that is how you will have to begin. I hesitated long over Mrs. Gamp. I knew she would bring rare insight and knowledge to the subject of liquor control, but her ideas on hygiene are at variance with modern notions. Nowadays you must bank on soap and eugenics. Mrs. Gamp is too staunch a Conservative for these degenerate days.

Then it flashed across me in a moment of inspiration : The woman candidate the world is waiting for is Rosa Dartle!

I had read carefully many election addresses of aspiring Parliamentary ladies and had come to the conclusion that they were not working on right lines. They seemed too content to copy the methods of mere man which have long been acknowledged failures. It is no use promising the weary voter obvious impossibilities. He is tired of the old game. The woman candidate must strike a new and feminine note of her own, else in vain is the net spread in the sight of the bird. I am certain, my dear niece, that if you, as a Parliamentary candidate, will model your political methods on the pretty ways of Miss Rosa Dartle you will score an instant success.

You have read your "David Copperfield" and will remember that Rosa "never said anything she wanted to say outright ; but hinted at it and made a great deal more of it by this practice." She always wanted to be put right if she was wrong and only asked for information, and in that ingenious way put forward her own views and corrected every idea opposed to her own. This she did with such power and skill that Steerforth and his mother with whom she lived were entirely unaware of her power, though Copperfield soon discerned that whilst she was thanking others for information she was really exposing the hollowness of their argument and laying down the true rule to her ignorant audience.

So that we can imagine if Rosa Dartle, M.P., were to be told by an eminent statesmen that in his view all the Labour Party were Bolsheviks, she would say : " Oh, but really ? Do tell me—are they, though ? " And when the Eminent One asseverated that Bolsheviks they were and in his opinion always had been and always would be, she would continue : " Really ! Well, I don't know, now, when I have been better pleased than to hear that. It's so consoling. It's such a delight to know that all the Labour leaders are really wicked scoundrels like Lenin and Trotsky. I had my doubts, I confess, but now they are cleared up. I thought you used to be quite friendly with some of them and ask them to tea—or was it breakfast ?—and I remember that made me quite uneasy. I used to think some of the Labour men helped to win the war and made sacrifices just like ourselves, and we used to think them such splendid fellows—when the war was on, I mean. But now I shall dismiss the idea of them altogether. And do you really think if they are Bolsheviks they will have a Red Army and shall we have a White Army ? How nice for everyone. And which Army do you think will win ? Because from what I heard about Russia——. But then you know and I don't. Live and learn. I didn't know, and now I do know, and that shows the advantage of asking—don't it ? "

Surely, Rosa, M.P., seated on the front Opposition bench always " asking for information, you know," would be a new and delightful figure in the political world spurring on the great ones of the earth to still more entertaining indiscretions.

I can imagine that Rosa might even have had some

success with that tiresome Old Lady of the Sea, Dora, who during the war was invited into the household by some foolish man just to help us over the week-end and seems to have settled down, bag and baggage, with us as a permanent housekeeper for the rest of her natural life. I think Rosa would have made this disreputable old political obliger inclined to look out for a new place.

For Miss Dartle would have asked her in a most winning manner why it was she could not buy a box of chocolates in the theatre? And when Dora snapped out that it was her way of winning the war, Rosa would say: "Oh! I am glad to know that. My dear Dora, it is kind of you to tell me that. And I suppose the Germans and the Turks did not eat chocolates in the theatre, and so they lost the war—and you won it. Or did the Eminent One win it?—I always forget. Or have we won it yet? And may we eat chocolates yet—I mean in the theatres? No, of course not. Now I'm glad to know that. I ask for information, and I'm glad to know it. Of course, if we went on eating chocolates in the theatres the war might start again. I quite understand. And of course the Chocolate Controller would lose his job? There is a Chocolate Controller, I suppose? Well, that's quite delightful to feel that, anyhow, he is safe. You can't think how happy it makes me."

And perhaps if poor old Dora had to stand up to Rosa every day of her life a few heart to heart talks of this nature would make her consider the advisability of packing up her remaining traps and leaving a household where she has long outstayed her welcome.

I can well imagine that Rosa, M.P., would have a few merry hours with Bureaucracy and certainly would not make its burden lighter. I can believe, for instance, that she would take an intimate interest in and want to know all about that forgotten Ministry of Supply.

" Why is it," she would ask, " that we are not going to have a Ministry of Supply, after all? I thought you told me only the other day it was so necessary and essential. But you know how ignorant I am. Still, didn't some Eminent One say we must have one—about a couple of years ago, I think? So now it's all altered. Well, I am glad. But do tell me why? Couldn't you find anyone to put on the staff? Of course you could. How foolish of me. What about all the poor fellows who wanted employment in it? Doesn't it seem a pity not to have a Ministry for them? And who will take care of that nice place near Windsor that you used to see from the railway—where all the lorries used to stand out in the open during the winter? It was done to harden them, wasn't it? I want to be put right if I'm wrong. But should you keep motors in the open, or why do some people have garages for them? So that is what is called 'running it commercially'? Well, I'm very glad to hear it. Now I know exactly what that means. Such a splendid example to the country. Now I know what to do. I shall never allow people to talk to me of wastefulness and profligacy and so forth in connexion with that place any more. Only isn't it a pity it is called Slough? It reminds one of 'Pilgrim's Progress.' What was that Slough called? But now I know, I shan't think of that any more. Thank you so very much."

It is possible that a few delicate showers of Rosa's interrogations would do more to penetrate the fleece of the woolliest Bureaucrat and damp the enthusiasm of his self-sufficiency than many thunderstorms of denunciation.

Our Eminent Ones would welcome Rosa. The blunt manners of their present critics and the want of trust and faith in their super-statesmanship pains them. Rosa's feminine charms would be at once kindly and efficient. The Eminent Ones would never suspect that she might be "pulling their leg," as the moderns phrase it. If they were to deprecate a too pointed question with: "Pray do not think, Miss Dartle——" She would eagerly interrupt with frank self-reproach: "I don't think. Oh, dear me, don't suppose that I think anything. I am not suspicious. I only ask a question. I don't state any opinion. I want to found an opinion on what you tell me. Then it's not so? Well, I am very glad to know it."

Consider this matter, my dear niece, very seriously, for I should not have put it forward to you unless I was convinced that as Rosa, M.P., I was casting you for a part that would bring sweetness and light into the question hour of the House of Commons and make you a box-office success at the Theatre Royal, Westminster. At the hustings, too, I am sure the rôle would play to votes. The free and independent are long since weary of the activities of The Honourable Samuel Slumkey and Horatio Fizkin, Esquire, and will flock to the poll to vote for Rosa Dartle. After a few months of pertinacity in the House I feel certain you will be offered at least a recordership, but it may be coupled with the condition that you must resign your seat.

Keep this great idea strictly to yourself, for I am sure you will find it of value to you when the time comes to enter the political arena. Meanwhile, continue diligent in your solemn studies, but also do not forget to make sacrifice to the Graces. As one of those who has always looked forward to welcoming Portia to the Courts I feel that now you have passed your Roman Law I can sing *Nunc Dimittis*.

Never forget that you are coming to a profession where there are great and honourable traditions and an unwritten law prescribing a high code of honour. I have no fear that the entry of women into the profession will in any way hinder the right course of its evolution. On the contrary, my hope is that you and your young friends will descend among us like angels of sweetness and light and teach us in ages to come a gospel of greater efficiency.

Your affectionate Uncle,

Dogberry.

Chapter XI : *Concerning Witchcraft and Wizardry*

I DO not remember that any barrister ever wrote a practical treatise on the Law in relation to witchcraft, yet just as we have Byles on Bills and other alliteratives and learned treatises on legal subjects so we might have expected Williams on Wizardry or Bacon on the Black Art. For well within two or three hundred years ago witchcraft and wizardry were practical legal subjects, and a prosecuting counsel who went Quarter Sessions had to be as well equipped in the law of witchcraft as in the law of larceny.

From a Christian point of view there has always been a sin of witchcraft, but not every sin is a legal crime, and though the sin of witchcraft is as prevalent as ever it was and necromancers flourish in our midst, it is no longer part of the common law of the land that witches and wizards should be burnt alive.

But in 1627, and for more than a century afterwards, when the Grand Jury met at Assizes or Sessions, bills would be presented against poor wretches charged with witchcraft and the judges would direct the Grand Jury on the law of the matter, pointing out in which cases it was advisable for them to find the bills and to send the prisoners for trial. It was in the year named, that the

Reverend Richard Bernard, vicar of Batcombe in Somerset, published his pleasant little treatise, " A Guide to Grand Jurymen in Cases of Witchcraft," which he diplomatically dedicated in the first place to two learned Barons of the Exchequer, and secondly to his friends the Archdeacon of Wells and the Bishop's Chancellor, to show that he had the approval of both the Law and the Church.

Many an honest magistrate must have risen from the study of this treatise with a troubled mind, for though warnings are given against hastily accepting all the perjuries and deceptions that were offered to juries by the malicious, bent upon the destruction of an unpopular neighbour, yet the existence of witches and wizards was stoutly contended for as a necessary complement to Christianity and part of the law of the land. Our reverend author tells us that " though the sober belief of good and bad spirits is an essential part of every good Christian's faith, yet imaginary communications with them have been the spring both of the worst corruptions of Religion and the greatest perversion of justice."

Bernard was a puritan preacher of God with a firm common sense, and saw that the real evil in the sin of witchcraft which still continues with us to-day was that form of necromancy which has always been a lure for the fool and a very present help to the knave, namely, the pretence that an individual has the magic power of calling up spirits from the vast and has the gift of holding communications with good or evil spirits.

And Bernard notes with curiosity what perhaps is still

true, that women are more addicted to witchcraft than men. Our author considers that that is due in a large measure to Satan's original success with Eve. He also holds the now discredited doctrine that women are more impatient and superstitious than men and, being displeased, more malicious and revengeful and, he adds, " more tongue-ripe and less able to hide what they know from others, and therefore in this respect are more ready to be teachers of witchcraft to others."

In spite of the passing of the Sex Disqualifications (Removal) Act, 1919, some may think that a faint aroma of truth continues to exhale from this old-world wisdom.

For my own part I think that the reason that there were more prosecutions for witchcraft than for wizardry arose mainly from the fact that the Grand Jury consisted wholly of men and were directed by judges who were also of the male sex, and these officials instinctively shrank from applying to a fellow-man those vague tests of crime that went to prove wizardry, having at the back of their minds an uneasy feeling that a charge of this kind might easily be made against one of themselves.

History tells us that when Laws or Religions want victims they take the weakest. The tender bodies of women and children have always been more seemly and acceptable sacrifices on the altars of the gods than a tough sixteen-stone man. Whether this is due to an accurate knowledge of the appetites of the immortals or to an unselfish diffidence in man himself it is hard to say, but the fact stares us in the face that in these matters the Law has always followed the line of least resistance.

Our forefathers took a stern view of those who by force of magic endeavoured to raise the Devil or pretended to hold communication with the dead.

They wisely condemned all such practices as harmful to the living and generally fraudulent in intent. But in practice it was found that mere severity did not destroy the evil and that, as far as the belief in witches and their ways was concerned, it was better to leave the affair to time and education rather than seek to cauterize it out of human nature with faggots and stakes.

In Society to-day you will not expect to hear stories told of any modern Countess such as were the common gossip of the Court of James I about the beautiful Frances Howard. For she was known to cross the river to Lambeth to visit her dear wizard, Dr. Forman, and persuade him to make waxen images of her lover and her husband that the former might become calid and the latter grow frigid, all of which the old rascal used to solemnly perform at great cost and little purpose for his fashionable employer.

But such coarse and futile wizardry no longer satisfies the appetites of fashionable idlers, and for many generations nowadays witchcraft and the Black Art and communications with spirits and the dead are practised through a medium, and though no doubt a certain amount of evil is caused to weak, unstable temperaments and some money passes from the purses of fools to the pockets of knaves, the Law wisely looks over the heads of these dabblers in necromancy unless its direct attention is drawn to them by actual fraud.

But in remote corners of our island you may still find

the old-fashioned practice of witchcraft as it was known to Richard Bernard and his grand jurors. A year or two ago there was a curious case came into Court in South Wales, where some gypsies obtained several hundred pounds from a simple farmer by persuading his wife that she and her son and her husband, as well as her house and all her goods and chattels, were bewitched and that the only cure for their condition was to hang round their necks bags of magic ashes which the gypsies sold to them at high prices. In a Staffordshire police-court a woman was fined for obtaining money by false pretences, having told an ex-soldier's wife that she had an evil spirit and sold to her what she called a " planet " in a parcel which was alleged to be a certain remedy for the terrible but imaginary condition of the patient. These are instances of the old crude Elizabethan witchcraft.

In the same way only a few years ago in Ireland some ignorant and misguided peasants actually burned one of their relatives on the ground that she was a witch, and they were tried and convicted of the murder. In Ireland and Wales a belief in the old witchcraft and wizardry is by no means uncommon to-day. I remember only a few years ago in a valley near Snowdon a Welsh farmer for several years refused to take the hay off an island in the river which belonged to the farm. His landlord remonstrated with his tenant in permitting the farmer on the opposite side of the valley coming down to his island and carrying off his hay. But no explanation could be obtained until at last the neighbour opposite left the county. Then the farmer boldly went on to his island and cropped it and informed his landlord that he had not dared to do it before as his neighbour was a wizard and had threatened to put the evil eye on his children and his cattle if he interfered with the meadow in any way. This was fully confirmed by many in the neighbourhood who, though devout attendants at chapel, firmly believed in wizardry and the power of the Evil Eye. There are still lots of wizards and witches in Wild Wales and in many other remote parts of our islands.

Nor can I see why we should be surprised to find that such beliefs still have some hold upon the human mind. It is less than three hundred years ago since Chief Baron Hale directed a Suffolk jury to find two poor old women guilty of witchcraft and assured them that witches undoubtedly existed since: "first the Scripture had affirmed so much, secondly the wisdom of all nations had provided laws against such persons which is an argument of their confidence of such a crime."

Now, Hale was a civilised and learned man, and arguments and beliefs held by him need not be scoffed at when they are found still existing in the minds of simple folk whose habits of body and mind have altered very little in the last three hundred years.

The Welsh are great readers of the Bible and regard its letter with peculiar reverence. Like good Richard Bernard, many of them no doubt devoutly hold the doctrine that the "sober belief of good and bad spirits is an essential part of every Christian faith," and since witches and wizards are mentioned in Holy Writ it would savour of impiety and throw doubt on the whole structure of Scripture if one might not believe in the contemporary magic of the Evil Eye.

Arguments of this nature which appealed to the minds of Chief Barons a few generations ago and were preached from high places to the populace cannot be suddenly uprooted from the minds where the good seed fell. Here and there you will find these flowers of legal thought still flourishing in remote pastures, for the world moves very slowly in our older counties. Official education, so called, is a comparatively modern business and not mentally stimulating. You will find the old traditions and folk-lore of the country-side alter only in geological periods of time and are scarcely affected by the passing of statutes and the change of fashion in intellectual circles.

Nor can the professors and well-to-do idlers who hold their witches' sabbaths in darkened drawing-rooms and hang on the words of a well-paid medium afford to point the finger of scorn at their bumpkin cousins who as loyal die-hards stand fast by the more ancient creeds. All these things are based on a tendency in the human mind to believe in magic. It is common to rich and poor, learned and simple. Every one of us has his moments of belief in some form of magic. You would think a Chancery Judge as immune as most human beings from this kind of thing, yet I have noticed one of these rare and learned beings deliberately change his seat at the bridge table to follow the luck of the cards.

Between a movement of this sort and witchcraft necromancy and the evocation of the spirits of the dead there is doubtless a wide gap, but they are all, I fancy, gestures of obeisance to the god of magic. For we are children of forgotten ages and follow faithfully in the footsteps of our forefathers. How modern is the story of Saul's visit to the lady medium at Endor. Saul, it must be remembered, had passed some excellent legislations to "cut off those that have familiar spirits and the wizards out of the land." But, like all measures for the prohibition of human folly, it was not likely to be successful, since even the legislators themselves hankered after the thing prohibited. Still, we must remember to Saul's credit that he did not break the law of his own land by patronising local talent, but, like many modern religious men, he went abroad to do that which he had caused to be forbidden in his own country. It is further to Saul's credit that he seems to have been thoroughly ashamed of visiting the lady medium of Endor, and so we read that he disguised himself and put on other raiment and came to the woman under cover of night. It must have been a disconcerting journey for a sensible man, and the picture of the legislator sneaking across Palestine in fancy dress and a second-rate make-up to consult one of the very riff-raff he had so wisely outlawed from his own country is far from dignified.

The display of the Endor medium was an excellent one and Saul, like all persons who desire to see and hear things, saw and heard what he wanted. The medium left nothing to chance. She knew all about her royal visitor and refused to start the séance until she was promised that there should be no police-court proceedings for breaking the law. The kingly word having been given, it is curious to read the account of the witch's procedure. Like the medium of to-day, the witch of Endor appears to go into a trance and hear voices and see visions. Saul does not at first perceive anything himself, but later on is easily persuaded that he has seen and heard a ghost, and the experience leaves him, as it leaves many a dabbler in modern witchcraft, in a condition of hysterical terror. It is amusing to read that the medium is at great pains to persuade Saul to stay to supper, as having been her guest it would be impossible for him to go back upon his word and hand her over to his Attorney-General. The king makes a night of it, and the story ends with a supper of fatted calf and new bread.

Here you have a record no doubt quasi-historical of a spirit séance which was undoubtedly treated as actual fact by many generations and maybe is still so regarded by some. There are to-day hundreds of individuals who will burden your ears with similar historical experiences if you have the patience to suffer them gladly. But believers in the magical practices and ritual of witchcraft have even better evidence than legends and stories in the actual evidence produced in Courts when witches, and more often wizards, turned King's evidence or, being convicted, confessed their crimes. Anne Whittle alias Chattox tells us in lurid detail how Elizabeth Southernes alias Demdike introduced her to the honourable society of witches.

The records of the Court show that " the devil appeared to her in the likeness of a man about midnight at the house of the said Demdike, and thereupon the said Demdike and she went forth of the said house unto him : whereupon the said wicked spirit moved this examinate that she would become his subject and give her soul unto him. The which at first she refused to assent unto ; but after by the great persuasion made by the said Demdike she yielded to be at his commandment and appointment. Whereunto the said wicked spirit then said unto her that he must have one part of her body for him to suck upon."

In this way did the Evil One put the seal upon his victims and the marks remained to be pointed out by professional witch-finders. Poor old Mother Chattox, blind and withered, chattering and muttering all this wonderful balderdash, is tried, convicted, and burned at Lancaster with a goodly crowd of others duly convicted to the satisfaction of judge and jury, who believe it all as gospel. And if these things satisfied the educated instincts of a few generations ago, who accepted them as proved truths and slew their victims to justify their beliefs, how can we marvel that foolish folk are still parting with their money to hired mediums on the same valuable consideration?

For we may take it, I fancy, that as long as there is money in the manifestation of magic so long will some sorts and conditions of magic find their way into the market. For many generations alchemy was a favourite hobby of the upper classes, who glibly fostered any quack who promised to manufacture gold for them. About a hundred years ago a Dr. Price of Guildford convinced a lot of credulous folf that he had succeeded in turning mercury into gold, but unfortunately committed suicide a few days before he should have shown his experiments to a committee of experts, and the secret died with him.

Astrology has been a universal science of quackery and

in its prime regulated the lives of men and the fate of nations, but it has fallen on evil days of late. Still, in obscure corners seedy professors of the science will earn a few shillings by casting a horoscope and promising prosperous matrimonial relations to their simple customers based on the fact that Saturn is well posited in the fifth house and the sextile of the sun is busying itself with the village idylls of Mary and John.

And the law which used to take a forbidding parental interest in witches, wizards, astrologers, mediums, and other makers of magic now gives them a free hand as long as they do not make use of their parlour tricks to cheat the simple, unsuspecting believer out of his money. It is a curious human trait that attracts the monied fool to the magic-maker, and he in turn, however clever and successful in the legitimate conjuring business, cannot keep his fingers out of his clients' pockets. These seem natural magnetisms similar to that of the candle for the moth. There is certainly nothing supernatural about the cheating medium. He is of the earth earthy. But doubtless there have been mediums, as there have been witches, who believed they had a divine mission. The curious trait in their faithful followers is that fraud has little effect on their faith.

One of the most remarkable of the fraternity in recent years was Daniel Dunglas Home. He might perhaps have been regarded as a self-deceiver and left a more or less clean and sainted memory behind him had he resisted the temptation of spoiling a half-witted old woman of her money and thereby found himself up against the laws of equity administrated by a Vice-Chancellor wholly emancipated from the spiritual direction of Home's familiars.

Daniel Dunglas Home was a rogue and a vagabond, direct descendant of the "Slight-of-hand Artists pretending to do wonders by virtue of Hocus Pocus the Powder of Pimper le Pimp or the like," for whom our forefathers prescribed stocks and whipping-posts. He played Autolycus to the aristocracy of the Victorian age, was a snapper-up of unconsidered trifles in every Court of Europe, for the fashionable world liked the rogue, flocked to him to be bamboozled, and were fooled to the top of their bent.

His career is a romance. Born in Scotland in 1833, said to be a natural grandson of the tenth Earl of Home with a Highland mother, gifted with second sight, he spends his childhood in America. He is delicate, nervous, and a seer of visions. Probably a hysterical child, unconscious in the first instance that he is deceiving himself and others, he is quickly drawn on to the downward path by the surrounding faithful who humoured and fondled him and magnified his childish miracles, and drank in his talk of signs and wonders and the invisible world.

He readily adopted the rôle of a professional medium and met with success from the first. At the age of twenty-two he came to Europe. America was already too provincial for his talent.

There was probably more money in the medium business in the fifties than there is to-day. The aristocracy and the idle hangers-on at continental Courts took it up as a change from cards and scandal. They had money to burn and plenty of spare time in which to burn it. The Courts have always been the great patrons of necromancy from the days of King Saul. An English lady of fashion writing from the Continent tells us that the great American medium "turns the world upside down." The Kings of Wurtemberg and Prussia welcome Daniel Dunglas to their Courts. British Ministers at Madrid, Vienna, and Constantinople throw open their *salons* to him and compete for his patronage.

His greatest triumph is in Russia, where he marries Alexandrina, daughter of Count de Kroll and god-daughter to the Czar Nicholas. Doubtless the fellow was a great lady-killer. Elizabeth Barrett Browning called him her "protégé prophet," and all the idle ladies in Florence sit fascinated at the rogue's feet.

Old Robert Browning sees him with other eyes:

> "Sweet and clean, dining daintily, dizened smart,
> Set on a stool buttressed by ladies' knees,
> Every soft smiler calling me her pet."

It reads like a survival of the worship of the Evil One by the poor uneducated witches in a country barn where, if you accept the records and the evidence, similar miracles to those of Home were continually exhibited, and as the Devil in his worship had more witches than wizards in his congregation so undoubtedly Home's successes were greater among women than men.

Even where men accepted his manifestations they instinctively distrusted his honesty. Hiram Powers, the American sculptor, a Swedenborgian who when living at Florence was greatly attracted by Home's miracles, "gives a decided opinion that he is a knave, but thinks him so organised nevertheless as to be a particularly good medium for spiritual communications." Nathaniel Hawthorne preferred not "to receive a message from a dead friend through the organism of a rogue," and could not force his mind to take any interest in the fashionable man of mystery. Browning, however, took a practical business interest in the fellow and, being utterly fed up and disgusted with his pretensions, sat down and wrote "Mr. Sludge the Medium," which is not only the last word about Daniel Dunglas and mediums and their dupes, but is a popular psychological study of the evolution of the medium and valuable to us to-day as showing clearly how grave a responsibility a man takes when he patronises a medium and induces a fellow-creature to continue a profession of deceit.

However, the human nature of rogues and fools being what it is, one must accept the inevitable, and I doubt if Home could possibly have run straight even if his friends and patrons had given him the chance. It is possible that to some extent he believed in his own powers, for the self-deception not only of dupes, but of the medium himself, is well recognised in the pathology of spiritualism.

Still, in his encounter with the Law he must have received a rude shock to his belief in the supernatural if, indeed, he was a believer. It has always seemed to me that the spirits who played accordions for Daniel Dunglas wafted him through dining-room windows in the sight of the faithful, enabled him to handle live coals, and generally assisted at his exhibitions, let him down very badly when he came before a court of Equity. A few respectable spirits, rapping out their evidence in the witness-box, might have saved our unfortunate hero £60,000 and costs.

The way of it was this. In October, 1866, Home, now aged thirty-three, was down on his luck. The publication of " Mr. Sludge " had not done him any good. His wife had died and her relations had brought an action about her property. The fashionable world was tiring of him, but he had a few faithful friends left, and, to relieve his pecuniary embarrassment, the Spiritual Athenæum was started at 22 Sloane Street with a hundred five-guinea subscribers, and Home, as Secretary, living on the premises.

A room in 22 Sloane Street is the first scene in the legal drama. Home the medium is discovered. He is a graceful and mysterious figure; a most distinguished-looking man, of the blonde type; has beautiful hands and feet, fine teeth, a good mouth, eyes that reflect the wisdom of the heavens, a voice rich and of large compass, uttering spiritual sympathy to the afflicted. A gifted creature. Byronic! A slightly shop-soiled Don Juan.

To him enter Mrs. Lyon. A foolish, vulgar old dame, lonely, obscure, and enormously wealthy. She, too, fancies herself as a medium. Has had her own trumpery, tin-pot spirit messages, so she says. She is fascinated by Home. Especially pleased with his glib talk of royal and aristocratic friends, being, like most dear old Victorian women, a thorough snob.

There are séances. The widow Lyon is informed by the spirit of her deceased husband that he is the father of Dan and "therefore Dan is your son!" The old woman relishes the idea of such a handsome son. Bestows on him a gift of £30 right away, and next day £50, and then proposes to adopt him, and he shall introduce her not only to new spirits from the vasty deep, but also to all his fashionable friends on this side of Jordan.

Events move rapidly. Within ten days the affair is settled. The half-cracked old lady sits down and writes her dear boy a letter expressing "her greatest satisfaction in now presenting you with and as an entirely free gift from me the sum of £24,000." The phrase "with and as an entirely free gift" suggests to me that if the old lady drafted her letter herself she was inspired by the spirit of a deceased attorney. Mrs. Lyon, in her evidence, declared that the suggestions came to her from her husband's spirit via the mediumship of Home. Next month the fascinating son is adopted. Daniel Dunglas Home becomes Daniel Dunglas Home-Lyon. He receives another £6000, and in January, 1867, another £3000. What wonderful spiritual gifts the fellow has!

There are many who still credit Daniel Dunglas with abnormal powers. I for one do not doubt he had qualities few of us possess. Within three months to charm £60,000 out of the purse of a miserly old widow of seventy-five and become her adopted son with expectations of another hundred thousand. This was "some" spiritualism!

Unfortunately, Home's dream did not last. He was a restless vagabond, and found the old lady peevish and tedious. "I have sold my liberty," he sighed, "and it is not a bed of roses." So, instead of trotting the old dame round to see his aristocratic friends in Mayfair he went off on his lonesome to Brighton and Torquay and Malvern for the sake of his health.

The old lady is naturally disgusted. She gets anxious at his continued absence, and when her dearly adopted writes to her that he is off to a German spa and suggests she should come with him to a far-off foreign land, her shrewd British maternal instinct is affronted. She fears she is to be deserted. She consults lawyers. A writ of *ne exeat regno* is issued. Home is arrested, and the next day is liberated on depositing in court the deed of gift.

The scene now shifts to the Court of Chancery. The story of *Lyon v. Home* is extant and writ in the quaint language of the Equity Reports. The trial in its day caused a buzz and a stir among the fashionable ones. Women thronged the Vice-Chancellor's Court, and Home was hero or villain according as one was a believer or unbeliever in his friends of the under-world.

Home lost much sympathy by setting up as a defence that the silly old woman had quarrelled with him and wanted her gifts back again because he refused to marry her. The tale was improbable; for though the widow was an absurd, fantastic creature, she had a certain narrow cuteness and was the sort of person who would have been inclined to have put up the banns before she put down the cash. The Court considered the suggestion was a calumny, and Home's counsel readily dropped the point. His client was wanting in chivalry or he would never have pleaded it.

In cross-examination the medium swore that he was the subject of mysterious movements over which he had no control. The spirits moved him about bodily in violation of the ordinary rules of gravity, and did the same with chairs and tables in his presence. Also he swore that spirits communicated with him by means of raps and spelt out messages through an alphabet. The way of it was that Home ran through the alphabet, and at the right letter the spirit gave a rap.

Upon this counsel suggested that an effort should be made to obtain evidence in this way from the spirit world on the subject-matter of the action.

" Give me a knock, if you please, Mr. Home," asked counsel, persuasively.

There was a dead silence in the court. A pause of moments. Never had the tricksy spirits such a chance of converting the world of unbelievers. Never had a devoted disciple and medium been in greater want of the support of his familiars. The shorthand writer sat breathless with poised pencil. The old judge dipped his quill in the ink. The tense silence grew insupportable. Not a rap! At length Daniel Dunglas shook his head.

" I cannot do so," he murmured.

The drama was over.

At the end of a long trial judgment was given by the Vice-Chancellor declaring the gifts to be fraudulent and void. No one greatly pitied the half-cracked old fool whose erratic folly had caused all the pother.

Nor did Daniel Dunglas lose many adherents, for his friends and followers continued to believe in those shy, elusive spirits who refused to be subpœnaed by worldly courts, but still played accordions and tilted tables in the drawing-rooms of wealth and fashion.

The story of Home is interesting as showing the limited power of the Law. The Law could set right the wrong done by the citizen Home against the citizen Lyon, but from the point of view of the faithful the decision has always been regarded as quite irrelevant to the supernatural powers of Home the medium.

In the same way the law that tried to put down witchcraft by burning, torture, and imprisonment was an utter failure, and probably by making martyrs of the witches did something to popularise their superstitions. The modern theory seems to be that the witchcraft of recent times was a survival from the ancient heathen religion of Western Europe and that the witches were really worshippers of the old gods. The prosecution of witches was therefore an attack on heresy, the outcome of the supremacy of the Christian religion. The priests of any dominant religion always seek to destroy their opponents and to use the law for that purpose, but with increasing civilisation law and lawyers have become shy of pulling chestnuts out of the fire for turbulent priests.

The Law recognises that there is a natural human tendency to sport with necromancy, witchcraft, wizardry, and all forms of magic which, though no doubt not as strong to-day as in the age of King Arthur, has a distinct existence like thirst for drink and gambling. These human tendencies cannot be restrained by legal penalties, though they may be modified by wise precept and sane example. The Law is never more beneficent than when it is tolerant and, the police should walk up and down outside the halls of magic and leave the professors and their pupils severely alone unless the Law finds the professor cheating his pupils or the pupils testing the professor's supernatural powers by swimming him in a duck pond. Then the Law should blow the whistle of judgment, restore order, and allow the game to proceed according to the old rules.

Chapter XII : *Concerning Rufus Choate*

RUFUS CHOATE was to America the typical great advocate. As Curran was to Ireland, as Erskine was to England, so was Choate to America; greater than Pinkney, Prentiss, Hoffman, or even Daniel Webster himself. Richard H. Dana voiced the feeling of the American Bar in a memorable tribute to his memory when he said: "The great conqueror, unseen and irresistible, has broken into our temple and has carried off the vessels of gold, the vessels of silver, the precious stones, and the ivory, and we must content ourselves hereafter with vessels of wood and stone and iron."

Rufus Choate was born in Ipswich, Massachusetts, in 1799, and died a barrister, having refused judicial honours, at the early age of sixty. From his youth upward he was devoted to advocacy. He lived for his profession, and never ceased to be an earnest student of his art. For him jurisprudence was, in Justinian's phrase, "the knowledge of things divine and human, the science of what is just and unjust." He was a very widely read man; but everything he learned and read he adapted to the uses of advocacy. He was enthusiastic in his love of his trade. He had often on his lips the words of Archbishop Hooker: "Of law no less can be said than that her seat is the bosom of God, her voice the harmony of the spheres; all things in heaven and earth do her reverence: the greatest as needing her protection, the meanest as not afraid of her power." When a young student remarked to him that the study of law became less dry as one learned to know more about it, and that a man might absolutely learn to like it, he replied with generous impatience: "Like it! there is nothing else to like in all the world."

Choate was, however, not only a natural and gifted advocate, but a man who had devoted every hour of industry to the profession he loved. From earliest school-days he was a great reader, doing little in the football field; and yet because of the lovable nature of the boy he was not separated from his schoolfellows through pedantry or conceit. Throughout life he would insist that "in literature you find ideas; there one should daily replenish his stock." He was a careful reader of the English Bible, and quoted from it constantly in speaking. All the speeches of the English orators were well known to him, and he regarded Grattan with great admiration, though Brougham he would not admit to be a real orator. He was equally widely read in history, poetry, and the classics. "Soak your mind with Cicero," was a favourite phrase of his in giving advice to the younger generation of law students.

But we must not suppose that these miscellaneous pursuits were indulged in to the neglect of his mistress, the Law. It is not easy to find in legal biography instances of greater devotion to the study of the law. He carried out Lord Eldon's maxim, and knew what it was "to live like a hermit and work like a horse" ; and both in length of hours and—what is of far greater importance—interest and attention to the meaning of what he read, he was a model student. Thus, when as a young man of twenty-four he entered the Courts, it was said of him that he was a "full-grown lawyer, jurist, advocate, and, more than all, *man* at the start."

He was a great believer in reading with a pen in hand, that notes might be made without delay of new discoveries. Literature he read for ideas, words and phrases to fill out and decorate his orations. Law he read as the foundation of his life-work with an energy and enthusiasm that never slackened. Only a few years before his death a friend found him poring over a folio. "I am reading over again Coke upon Littleton," he said. "He is an enthusiast in the old law, and I want him to inspire my enthusiasm ; for it would be dreadful, you know, to lose one's interest in the profession to which a man is going to devote the last ten years of his life." One cannot picture to oneself an advocate of to-day burnishing his well-to-do wits with Coke upon Littleton.

The stories of the industry and energy of Rufus Choate are very inspiring, but they do not solve for us the interesting problem of the sources of his power as an advocate. The advocate, like the actor, passes out of the world's ken when his last speech is made. Now and then you get one of the audience gifted, like Charles Lamb, to describe to you in a few words what the actor really was like, and his portrait remains for all time. Such records are rare about actors, and still rarer about advocates. You have their reported speeches; but the method of delivery, the voice, gesture, and soul, whereby the advocate endowed his speech with life, beauty, and force—these things can only be gathered by our own imagination through dull second-hand histories.

Of the personal appearance of an advocate something may be learned by portraits or engravings. I feel sure that it is advisable for an advocate to be good-looking, and therefore I feel sure Rufus Choate must have been good-looking in some kind of way, though the pictures I have seen of him are not convincing. That he had a striking personality is undoubted. "No one who ever saw him could ever forget him," was said of him more than once. Edward Parker, his faithful pupil, writing with Sancho-like fidelity of the fascinating beauty of his youth, speaks of "that dark, Spanish, Hidalgo-like head, covered with thick raven curls, which the daughters of the black-eyed races might have envied; and the flash of his own sad eyes, sad but burning with Italian intensity."

From this portrait we may turn to the rough caricature of a Yankee "down-easter," if we desire to see something of the advocate himself as he appeared to the crowd at the back of the court who flocked in to listen to his orations:

"Rufus Choate is a picture to look at, and a crowder to spout. He is about seven feet six, or six feet seven, in his socks, supple as an eel, and wiry as a corkscrew. His face is a compound of wrinkles, 'yaller janders,' and jurisprudence. He has small, keen, piercing black eyes, and a head shaped like a mammoth goose-egg, big end up; his hair black and curly, much resembling a bag of wool in 'admirable disorder,' or a brush-heap in a gale of wind. His body has no particular shape; and his wit and legal 'dodges' have set many a judge in a snicker, and so confounded jurors as to make it almost impossible for them to speak plain English.

"Rufus is great on twisting and coiling himself up, squirming around, and prancing, jumping, and kicking up the dust, when steam's up. His oratory is first-rate; and his arguments ingenious and forcible. He generally makes a ten-strike (in America, the game of nine-pins being prohibited, the game of ten-pins took its place: a 'ten-strike' is a ball that knocks down all the pins. Hans Breitman refers to the joy of making a ten-strike) —judge and jury down—at the end of every sentence. He is great on flowery expressions and high-falootin' 'flub-dubs.' Strangers mostly think he is crazy, and the rest scarcely understand what it is about. He has been in the Senate, and may be, if he has time to fish for it, President of the United States. He invoices his time and eloquence four thousand per cent over ordinary charges for having oneself put through a course of law. Rufus Choate is about fifty years of age; perhaps over. He is considered the ablest lawyer in the United States."

The writer of this was evidently a man of discernment, for if there were a weak point in Choate's advocacy it was his fondness of "flub-dubs," if, as I gather, these are high-sounding words of low-sense power. He delighted in "long-tailed words in -osity and -ation," and these he would drag in, however humble the theme on which he was speaking. Moreover, alliteration had a great fascination for him. Thus, on a celebrated occasion in a very trumpery case he described some harness that his client had sold as " a safe, substantial, suitable, second-rate, second-hand harness." Albert Terrell, a decadent whom he defended for murder, was " this fond, foolish, fickle, fated, and infatuated Albert."

But one must not suppose these are fair samples of his style. The English of his orations is generally pure and of a literary flavour. He began in the true school. At a very early age—some say six years old—he could recite pages of " Pilgrim's Progress " and chapters of the Bible Throughout his life he read, as we have said, pen in hand in order to increase his vocabulary and add to his knowledge of language. A speaker, he thought, should " daily exercise and air his vocabulary and seek to add to and enrich it." He was a great classical scholar, and well read in literature ; but he had also a love of dictionaries, and would study them for the purpose of " filling up and fertilising his diction." These experiments led him into strange, verbal adventures.

A good story is told of one Mr. Justice Wilde, who, being dry, precise, and formal in his methods, little appreciated the whirlwind eloquence of Choate. On one occasion, just before the opening of Court, when Choate was to argue a case and they were waiting for him, a member of the Bar asked the Judge if he had heard that Mr. Worcester had just published a new edition of his dictionary with a great number of additional words in it.

"No!" replied Mr. Justice Wilde, "I have not heard of it. But for Heaven's sake don't tell Choate."

But although the exuberance of his verbosity was at times wearisome to his professional brethren, the juries were never tired of listening to him, and the public crowded in to hear his speeches. He laboured all his days to obtain the full feeling and sense of words spoken in advocacy, and the testimony of those who heard him is overwhelming that to have been in Court with Rufus Choate when, to use his own phrase, he "got his throat open," must have been a glorious experience.

There was no following in his footsteps, and many tried to discount the moral effect of his flights of eloquence by a studied humility of style. The best instance of such an effort was an opening by one Jeremiah Mason, a witty member of the Bar, who, when Choate after a magnificent oration had thrown himself exhausted on the bench, arose with blunt, homely, smiling cunning, and in a broad accent said: "Gentlemen of the jury, I don't know as I can *gyrate* afore you as my brother Choate does; but I want to just state a few pints."

Choate was a great defender of prisoners. He had none of that hesitation that has burdened the minds of some advocates as to how far it was the duty of an advocate to undertake a case he did not believe in. In his view "a counsel ought not to think anything about or know anything about whether his client is right or not; he ought only to think what can legitimately legally be said for him—what, according to the accepted principles of our law, is the legal defence." In this he followed the principles of Brougham and Erskine. But though of sturdy independence and no respecter of persons, in his attitude towards the Bench and his opponents, especially his juniors, he was a model advocate. Until the case was actually opened he was a most uncertain starter, and his juniors' chief and most arduous duty was to get him into Court. Once there, and when like a tiger he had tasted blood, nothing would drag him from the contest.

Records say, and probably with truth, that he was a wonderful advocate with juries. His methods were sound, and a young advocate might do worse than read and consider his ways. The jury to him was the elemental substance of a real trial. He cherished with tenacious affection the origin, history, and functions of a jury—in which matters he was nobly learned. He loved to discourse on the necessity of the agreement of the twelve, the presumption of innocence, the right of cross-examination, and the open hearing in Court with almost theological fervour. It was small wonder, then, that the actual twelve men he addressed found themselves transubstantiated from twelve common men into a great social and historic entity. As one writer says: "He did not argue very many great cases, but he made many little ones great." For the keynote of his success in advocacy was his eternal sincerity—a deep, great genuine sincerity. When this and his natural and acquired gifts are once understood, passages descriptive of his speaking that sound like hyperbole may be indeed even short of the truth.

The Reverend Dr. Hitchcock, President of the Union Theological Seminary in New York, whose friendship with Choate began in the pleasant hunting-ground of an antiquarian book-store, has left behind a fine picture of the charm of his eloquence.

"Certainly," he writes, "Rufus Choate seldom failed to carry his point with any jury, or any popular assembly. He caught men up and swept them along, as the wind sweeps leaves and dust. Whoever seeks to know the secret of this will find it pre-eminently in the innermost essential character of the man. He was pure, and just, and true, and tender, so that whatever he said commended, and still commends, itself to what is best and highest in our common nature. He was not only thoroughly good, but his goodness was fine and chivalric. The fascination was moral. The heart was captured first, and after that the imagination. His marvellous fertility of invention, wealth of allusion, and swift succession of inimitable felicities of thought and diction never seemed like devices to blind and betray the judgment, but came as naturally as the bloom of fruit-trees, or the foam of crested waves. His voice was one of a thousand, of ten thousand rather, now like a flute for softness, and now like a clarion."

One of his wise sayings to his younger friends was: "That in a speech to a jury the first moments were the great moments for the advocate. Then the attention is all on the alert, the ears are quicker, the mind receptive." A jury, he urged, at the beginning want to know what your case is about; they try and get hold of your leading notion. At the outset you want to strike into their minds a good solid general view of your case. To those who have watched a jury, all eagerness at first, dropping their attention as they are overwhelmed with dates and facts and extracts from letters instead of a broad statement of the case, Choate's advice seems worth recalling. "If," he said emphatically, "you haven't got hold of them, got their convictions at least open, in your first half-hour or hour, you will never get at them at all." Truly Choate had much to teach that some of us have still to learn.

In the same way he had a real detestation of riding several horses at once and never quite knowing which he was on. In every case he sought after the real point of the case, and had one central commanding theory. Then in weaving and winding the threads of facts he made his theory the hub around which everything had to revolve. This, too, is an eternal fact of advocacy which is apt to be forgotten in these hustled days.

As a cross-examiner, too, he had the gist of the matter in him. He never assaulted a witness or browbeat him, well understanding human nature and knowing that by unmannerly violence he would only arouse sympathy in the minds of the jury with the witness rather than the advocate. But he had his own methods of dealing with the evil doer, and of one such it is told us that "he did not call him hard names, but covered him over with an oily sarcasm so that the jury did not care to look at him. In other words, he was slain politely and laid out to dry."

Like all great cross-examiners, he never asked many questions. As he told a student: "Never cross-examine more than is absolutely necessary. If you don't break your witness he breaks you; for he only repeats over in stronger language to the jury his story. Thus you only give him a second chance to tell his story to them. And besides, by some random question you may draw out something damaging to your own case. This last is a frightful liability." Yet how often do members of the Bar cheerfully ruin their clients by a slovenly cross-examination without even the plausible excuse of youth and inexperience!

And another sound truth in matters of cross-examination which he put with amusing exaggeration to a favourite junior is worth remembering. "Let me," he said, with humorous solemnity, "give you my dying advice—never cross-examine a woman. It is of no use. They cannot disintegrate the story they have once told; they cannot eliminate the part that is for you from that which is against you. They can neither combine, nor shade, nor qualify. They go for the whole thing; and the moment you begin to cross-examine one of them, instead of being bitten by a single rattlesnake, you are bitten by a whole barrelful. I never, excepting in a case absolutely desperate, dare to cross-examine a woman." It was another wise American who said: "Live always in the fear of God; but if that slides, continue in the fear of Woman."

Of course, on occasion Choate would meet with his Sam Weller. Defending a prisoner for theft of money from a ship, a witness was called who had turned State's evidence and whose testimony went to prove that Choate's client had instigated the theft.

"Well," asked Choate, "what did he say? Tell us how and what he spoke to you."

"Why," said the witness, "he told us there was a man

in Boston named Choate and he'd get us off if they caught us with the money in our boots."

But Choate was not the man to grumble at an occasional knock, especially if it were a witty one, for he dearly loved a jest, and was brimful of wit and humour, which he could use himself with good effect.

In a case tried before a judge of the United States District Court, Choate, in his address to the jury, alluded to certain rumours as set afloat by a party's enemies.

" You mustn't assume that, Mr. Choate," interrupted the Court ; " there's no evidence that he has enemies."

" He's in large business and must have made foes," said Choate impatiently.

" There's no evidence," replied the judge, " that he's in business. He's a physician."

" Well, then," replied Choate instantly, with a roguish smile, " he's a physician, and the friends of the people he's killed by his practice are his enemies."

And as the laughter of judge and all in court died away Choate was returning to the matter in hand and pressing forward his point.

You could fill a book of anecdotes with Choate stories, but these tales of bygone wit baldly remembered seem too often to have lost their savour. One wants the voice and the manner, the accent and occasion of their utterance.

I like that saying of his about Judge Shaw : " I always approach Judge Shaw as a savage approaches his fetish : knowing that he is ugly, but feeling that he is great."

That is distinctly witty to-day; but how delightful it must have been to have known Judge Shaw and to have heard Rufus say it in the robing-room!

He seems to have had the Charles Lamb touch in some of his quaint, inverted thoughts of wit. Coming into a lawyer's office, he saw a narrow, winding staircase leading up to the consulting-room. He looked wonderingly at its corkscrew curvings, and, turning to the lawyer, meditatively observed: "Dear me! How drunk a man must be to go up those stairs!"

Again, at a season of illness, a friend of Choate visited him and urged him to pay more attention to his health.

"Sir," said the visitor, "you must go away; if you continue your professional labours, you will certainly undermine your constitution."

Choate looked up with grave irony and replied: "Sir, the constitution was destroyed long ago; I am now living under the by-laws."

And of the rougher American humour he had his share, too. Speaking to some young advocates of the misery of losing cases, he told them they must remember their ministerial positions and accept defeat philosophically and be ready to go on with the next.

"When a case has gone against me," he said, "I feel like the Baptist minister who was baptizing in winter a crowd of converts through a hole made in the ice. One brother—Jones, I think—disappeared after immersion and did not reappear: probably he had drifted ten or fifteen feet from the hole and was vainly gasping under ice as many inches thick. After pausing a few minutes the minister said : 'Brother Jones has evidently gone to Kingdom Come : bring on the next'!"

Of Choate the citizen many interesting things might be written in praise of his works and days, but this is only an attempt to picture Choate the advocate, and the best triumphs of advocacy are largely beyond the power of literary recall. We read of Rufus Choate as he "strode the streets with majestic step," we accept in faith the records of the marvellous music of his voice, the flashing glance of his dark eye and his bewitching smile, but we must sadly own that these memories of hearsay are not evidence and scarcely bring conviction to our legal minds.

This, however, we can ascertain—that in Rufus Choate we have for all time the example of a noble advocate. Ruskin tells us that "the chords of music, the harmonies of colour, the general principles of the arrangement of sculptured masses have been determined long ago and in all probability cannot be added to, any more than they can be altered." And if this be true of the greater arts it is certainly not untrue of advocacy. Rufus Choate devoted his life to the study of the principles of the great profession he adorned, and, without foregoing any liberty that genius and originality suggested to his mind, kept steadily before him the duties and limitations of the art of which he was a master. Doubtless there have been more outstanding figures at the Bar, men of greater position and larger influence. There has been none that I have read of who brought to his work a wider love and a more noble industry. His enthusiastic affection for all that his profession meant to him is best expressed in his own words to a friend who begged him in his last illness to take a vacation.

"Ah, my dear fellow!" he said, with playful sadness, "the lawyer's vacation is the space between the question put and the answer."

Chapter XIII : *Concerning Jumbo in Chancery*

AN elephant in a Chancery Court may seem at first blush to be as much out of place as a bull in a china shop. But " Jumbo "—as the astute Mr. Barnum said to himself—was some elephant.

Barnum coveted Jumbo, the largest African elephant in the world. The great showman dangles £2000 before the Committee of the Zoological Society. The hard-faced, wooden-hearted men on the Committee stretch out their hands for the money-bags. Jumbo is sold! Jumbo who has carried generations of metropolitan children in his big howdah! Jumbo the friend of our youth who shared our buns out of paper bags! Jumbo whom we loved and honoured! Just for a handful of silver he leaves us sorrowing—unless, indeed, the Law can help us!

For when the terrible truth filtered slowly through the long ears of the British public, and the horror of it filled their generous hearts, a great wave of indignation swept the country the like of which has never been witnessed before or since. From the throne to the garret protests were addressed to the Committee. Even John Ruskin protests! One question, and one question only, dominates the thoughts and talk of the people and the columns of the Press. Can this wrong be undone? Can Chancery save Jumbo?

There is, of course, nothing strange in an animal playing a part in a drama. Vincent Crummles's chaise pony used to "walk on," you remember, in "Timour the Tartar." Other animals have done the same. But Jumbo, as far as I know, is the only animal which ever played a star part in a legal drama and had a Chancery motion all to himself.

Technically the law regarded Jumbo as a chattel. The law never moves with the times. Not so long ago the law regarded slaves and even wives as chattels. It was this aspect of the law that prompted Mr. Bumble to remark "The law is an ass." To the children of the world, and to those grown-ups who still had the hearts of little children, Jumbo was a national institution, a universal pet, a friend of the family, and a domiciled Englishman.

Born in Abyssinia, Jumbo was captured in 1861 by Hamran Arabs on the banks of the Settite river. He was then a youngster about four feet high. They sold him to Johann Schmidt, a Bavarian collector, who brought him to the Italian Zoo. Thence he goes to the Jardin des Plantes, and in a moment of inspiration the Committee of our Zoo do a swap with the Frenchmen, giving them an old rhinoceros in exchange for young Jumbo. So he comes to the land of his adoption a little orphan elephant about five years old.

It is now 1882. Jumbo is coming of age, and getting a little unruly, perhaps, now and again, as young fellows will do. He is the largest elephant in the world—more or less—weighs some six tons, and is rather addicted, so his keepers say, to gluttony in the shape of buns—friendship's offerings—which, coupled with want of exercise are bad for the liver.

Shame it is to England that the mere reported fact of the sale of Jumbo, even the news that a box on wheels had been made to carry him to the steamer, roused no immediate anger in the people. But it was smouldering there, ready to blaze.

The drama opens with a scene in the Zoo so full of beauty and pathos that the eloquent reports of it in the daily Press make strong men weep and drive women and children distracted. Jumbo is in his house, unaware of any treachery. They come one February morning and put strong chains round his legs. He is suspicious, but having faith in his keepers says nothing. The female elephant in the next cell, Alice, Jumbo's little wife, is painfully agitated over the business and cries piteously as they manacle her lord and master and lead him away.

In the gardens stands a large cage on wheels. They bring Jumbo towards it. He hears little Alice whimpering in the distance. He trumpets aloud to her as much as to say, "Be of good cheer! I remain!" He refuses to enter the box on wheels. His keepers lead him back to his old house. Alice greets him with merry gambols and grunts a satisfaction.

Scene I.—Daybreak in the gardens. The cold, misty grey dawn of a London February. The authorities have decided that Jumbo should walk to the docks. His keepers lead him out of his house. They take him past the Parrot House to the gate. But at the very threshold a strange thing occurs. Jumbo stops and trembles. He utters low moans. The affectionate creature embraces, with his trunk, Scott, his favourite attendant. Scott at duty's call begs him to move forward. Alice is heard weeping "off." Jumbo kneels to his keeper in dumb despair. Scott urges him to rise and follow him into the Outer Circle. Jumbo shakes his ears, rolls slowly on his side, and lifting up his head trumpets out with fine indignation that the answer is in the negative.

This was the trunk call for help, the S.O.S. that got through and brought the British nation to his side.

For four weeks Jumbo is the centre-piece of English life. Thousands flock to the gardens to see him, murmur a fond farewell, and mingle their tears with those of the faithful Alice. The Queen telegraphs to the Committee. The Prince of Wales telegraphs. Hundreds of men, women, and children from all parts of the British Isles send letters and parcels of buns and sweets to Jumbo himself. The papers are crowded out with correspondence. "A Clergyman" denounces "this cruel and inhuman bargain." "Minnie," "Ada," "Maud," and "Jummy's Little Friend" send their sixpences for his defence.

A wise doctor in Harley Street collects subscriptions. Romer, Q.C., is retained. Legal opinions are taken, and the world hears with relief that a notice of motion is served and that for the moment at least Jumbo is safely in Chancery.

Simple citizens who got their notions of Chancery from "Jarndyce v. Jarndyce," imagined that "*re* Jumbo" would go droning along for years, and meanwhile their old friend would remain in the gardens. Alas! the days of Lord Eldon are gone. The motion turns out to be really a motion and moves apace.

To the plain man, too, it seemed a monstrous injustice that while Barnum, the American showman, was made a party to the action, Jumbo, our own inimitable Jumbo, remained a stranger to the suit. Being, as I have said, a chattel in the eyes of the law, Jumbo could not be a party to an action. You could not even endow Jumbo with a fund and make him a ward in Chancery. With this absurd result, that Jumbo, the real hero of the legal drama, was never heard at all and was not even allowed to put his trunk to an affidavit.

Another clever suggestion made at the time was not acted upon, and here Gladstone, who was then Prime Minister, was undoubtedly to blame. It was pointed out that Caligula, the Roman Emperor, had made his horse a consul. If this precedent had been followed and Jumbo had been made a Minister without portfolio, the Courts would probably have held that the sale of a Cabinet Minister to an American freak show was against public policy and Jumbo would have remained with us. Even if Jumbo had sat on the Cabinet many thought that it would have done no harm.

As it was, the case for an injunction to restrain the removal of Jumbo turned on charters and by-laws and the rights of a committee to sell "surplus stock"—an offensive phrase which grated on the susceptibilities of the elephant's best friends. Mr. Justice Chitty in refusing an injunction recognised that there was a moral and national side to the transaction, upon which he would not adjudicate. It was a misfortune that the case could not have been tried by a jury. No jury would have decided against Jumbo. But Chancery could not save him. Chancery was tried and found wanting.

The final scenes of the drama were perhaps less dignified. Children thronged the gardens to share their last buns with Jumbo, who over-ate himself disgracefully. His neighbours in the Zoo were neglected and grew soured and jealous. The Bactrian camel stood hungrily sneering over his garden rails at the crowds round the elephant house. The brown bears climbed their poles and swung open-mouthed towards the children who hurried along towards Jumbo.

Grave disapprobation, too, was expressed at the conduct of Alice when it was heard that, bribed by a bun, she had been trotting in and out of the travelling cage to decoy Jumbo to his fate.

Jumbo himself remained a hero to the end. With dignified resignation he retired from the contest, loyally accepting the judgment of Chitty, J., and stepping into his box of his own free will. It was felt that he had set us all a noble example of law-abiding loyalty which we ourselves must follow if we were worthy to be Jumbo's friends.

On March 23 a strange procession was formed. Since the days when popular victims made the last journey to Tyburn nothing like it is recorded. Ten of Pickford's strongest horses were fastened to Jumbo's car. Down Albany Street, along the Euston Road, through Clerkenwell to Tower Hill, and so to the Docks, Jumbo, followed by crowds of friends in carriages, in hansoms, and on foot, drives on in triumph. A good lady who had followed him with tears in her eyes provides him with copious draughts of beer for his breakfast ; another admirer gives him a nip of whisky.

His cage is swung carefully into a lighter, which drops down the tideway to the *Assyrian Monarch*, in which vessel his passage has been taken. The quays are thronged with cheering friends, crowds of boats follow the lighter with its precious freight, and a hundred sirens and steam-whistles echo the trumpet calls of Jumbo's farewell.

Such was the passing of Jumbo. Love, friendship, and honour were weighed in the scale against contracts and by-laws.

Chancery failed us.

Chapter XIV : *Concerning What the Archon Did*

IT is a comfortable theory among the middle classes that imprisonment for debt is abolished. They remember "Little Dorrit" and know that the Marshalsea is pulled down, and believe that imprisonment for debt went with it. For their own class it has been abolished since 1869, but Parliament deliberately retained it as a good discipline for the poor. The spendthrift of the aristocracy may fling other people's thousands about and waste his own substance in riotous living, but when the day of reckoning comes he planks down ten pounds and a humble petition (in bankruptcy), and a kindly Registrar begs him go forth and sin again, if he feels inclined to, at the end of two years.

But if a man on a weekly wage is improvident or unfortunate and runs into debt for a few pounds, a County Court Judge commands him to pay the debt at so many shillings a month, and if he does not pay owing to more improvidence or more misfortune, and it is shown that he has had, since the day the order was made, any means by which he could have paid, then he goes to gaol. At least, he ought to go to gaol, according to law, but it must be sorrowfully admitted that County Court Judges, being human beings, generally give him further time to pay, so that he may try to earn the money, or at least save it up out of earnings that ought to go in food for his family. If he continues out of work, then, when the bailiff comes with a warrant in his hand, it is most probable that a father, uncle, sister, cousin or aunt, or some neighbour equally poor as himself, will be blackmailed by the law and a sense of pity into paying his debt, and the costs, and the fees, that the State demands for keeping the system going, rather than allow a fellow-creature to go to gaol.

And the evil this does is not so much that a few bread-winners are taken to gaol and homes broken up, but that habits of improvidence are encouraged, reckless credit is given, extravagance and waste are stimulated, and a large class of undesirable knavish trades—tallymen, money-lenders, flash jewellery touts, sellers of costly family Bibles in series, gramophones and other luxuries of the mean streets—are enabled to foist their wares—a foister is good old English for a cheat—on poor folk whose character and worth in the world are injured by the evil *sequelae* of duplicity and shiftiness that are the common after symptoms of the degrading disease of debt.

And if you ask an ordinary citizen why this should not be swept away he tells you with a serious face that if it were swept away the poor man would not get credit for necessaries in his hour of distress. It is no use telling him that the only asset a working man has to which credit can be given is character, and that to allow him to mortgage his future earnings by pledging his body cannot be good for the community. The more hopeful argument, I find, is to point out to the pious citizen that to-day a betting man or even a publican will give credit on occasion to a working man whose character he knows, but generally these well-conducted businesses are cash businesses.

This being so, if a man wants to bet or wants to drink beer, he pays cash, and he on occasion wastes his substance on these things and makes too big a hole in his week's wages for one afternoon's amusement, because he relies on the credit so freely given by the "wicked grocer." If, on the other hand, the grocer were on a compulsory cash basis, too, a thoughtful working man might see well to make him a first mortgagee on the inadequate weekly wage. At present he is a very ordinary shareholder indeed, and too often only gets a meagre dividend under an order of Court, though no doubt he takes all this into account in the prices he charges. However we look at it, it is pleasant to know that, in spite of the absence of the sanction of imprisonment for debt, the businesses of betting men and brewer are by no means bankrupt, and the working man probably deals as much with both of them as is good for him. The system of imprisonment for debt, when you understand it, gives them a distinct pull over the grocer, and of course in any case we must admit that only the poor and most unfortunate of the poor go to prison. In times of good trade, and when the judicial temperament is less exacting and Spartan than it was, the number decreases.

During the war, when work and wages were plentiful and the women and children of those who were fighting were taken care of financially, imprisonment for debt very nearly abolished itself. In 1913, 5711 citizens were actually imprisoned for small sums of debt and costs. In 1919 the figure dropped to 206. But it is rapidly rising again. The touts and tallymen who were employed on national service have returned to their trails, the poor Registrars and High Bailiffs are no longer starving. The old credit system is at work amongst us again. The old vicious circle of poverty, credit, debt, costs, prison and more poverty, continues with us. Since 1869 over 300,000 citizens have gone to gaol for no other crime than that of poverty, or, as the middle-class Pharisee would prefer to call it, improvidence. But until it is understood, as men like Bramwell and Jessel recognised and explained to us, that imprisonment for debt is itself a cause of poverty and improvidence the vicious circle will roll on to eternity.

It is impossible to interest the average legislator about social matters that really matter. I am convinced that our bureaucrats and publicists will never be convinced of the necessity of the abolition of imprisonment for debt. Business interests think unlimited credit good for trade. Labour is supine, remembering credit is useful for strikes and lock-outs. For my part I have long since ceased to waste my time arguing about the matter. The abolition of imprisonment for debt is one of those obvious pieces of right action that you cannot argue about. I always preface anything I have to say concerning it with the Lancashire phrase, "Aw'm not argyin'—Aw'm tellin' thee." But there are some who won't be told, and to convert these it might be well to show them cinematographically, or historically if you will, what has been done in the past. This brings me to What the Archon Did.

Concerning What the Archon Did

The particular Archon I refer to is Solon.

Solon knew all about imprisonment for debt, and his evidence on the subject is most convincing. It is well to remember, too, that Solon was a business man—I have this from Grote, who got it, I fancy, from Plutarch Exekestides, Solon's father, a gentleman of the purest heroic blood, " diminished his substance by prodigality " and young Solon had to go into business; in modern phrase, " he went on the road," and saw a lot of the world in Greece and Asia. I mention this because I am always told that if I knew anything of business I should understand the necessity of imprisonment for debt. Solon was emphatically a business man. Solon was also a poet, which perhaps was his best asset as a social reformer, but he was no sentimentalist if, as some say, when he was a general attacking a rebellious city he ordered the wells to be poisoned to put an end to the strife. That at least showed that he could think imperially.

When Solon in a time of grand social upheaval was made Archon, he found the poorer population, including particularly the cultivating tenants, weighed down by debts and driven in large numbers out of freedom and into slavery. Let me set down the condition of things in the careful words of Grote, lest I appear to exaggerate:

" All the calamitous effects were here seen of the old harsh law of debtor and creditor—once prevalent in Greece, Italy, Asia, and a large portion of the world—combined with the recognition of slavery as a legitimate status, and of the right of one man to sell himself, as well as that of another man to buy him. Every debtor unable to fulfil his contract was liable to be adjudged as the slave of his creditor, until he could find means either of paying it or working it out ; and not only he himself, but his minor sons and unmarried daughters and sisters also, whom the law gave him the power of selling. *The poor man thus borrowed upon the security of his body* (to translate literally the Greek phrase) and upon that of the persons in his family."

The words I have italicised are interesting as exactly defining the principle of all imprisonment for debt. A wage-earner to-day who runs up bills with tallymen and grocers obtains credit upon the security of his body.

I have heard from the wife of a poor debtor an apt but unconscious translation of the Latin maxim, *Si non habet in aere luat in corpore*. Her allegation was that a tallyman had said to her husband, " If I canna 'ave yer brass I'll tek yer body." In the North country, among the more old-fashioned bailiffs and their victims, warrants of arrest are commonly known as " body warrants." No doubt the imprisonment of to-day is different in degree from the slavery of debtors in Greece five hundred years before Christ, but it is absolutely the same in principle, founded on the same idea, and worthy to be maintained or abolished by the citizens of this State for the same reasons that were found good by the citizens of Athens.

Thus it is that it is worth while finding out what Solon thought about it. I wish Solon's tract, " What the Archon Thought," had come down to us, and we could have quoted actual instances of the wickedness of imprisonment for debt in his day, but at least we know what he thought of it, and, what is really important to us, what he did. Solon had a pretty wit in titles. He called his bill *Seisachtheia*, or the shaking off of burdens. The relief which it afforded was complete and immediate. It cancelled at once all those contracts in which the debtor had borrowed on the security of his person or his land; it forbade all future loans or contracts in which the person of the debtor was pledged as security; it deprived the creditor in future of all power *to imprison* or enslave or extort work from his debtor, and confined him to an effective judgment at law, authorising the seizure of the property of the latter.

Here was indeed a shaking off of burdens. For we find that not only was imprisonment for debt abolished lock, stock, and barrel, but a law was enacted protecting the land of the cultivator from being seized for debt. This is akin to what in some of our colonies is called a homestead law, and I have always contended that in the interests of the State the few sticks of furniture which a poor man and his wife and children always call "the home" should be protected from arrest for debt, just as the breadwinner's body should be exempt from imprisonment. I could have got along with Solon.

And when one is told the old tale that has always been put forward by those who wish to retain imprisonment for debt—that the workman will starve for want of necessary credit and that trade will stagnate owing to timid creditors refusing to trade—let us remember with pleasure that that was not what the Archon saw as a result of his beneficial measures. On the contrary, the testimony is overwhelming that there grew up a higher and increasing respect for the sanctity of contracts. The system of credit-giving, and especially of money-lending, assumed a more beneficial character, and " the old noxious contracts, mere snares for the liberty of a poor free man and his children "—the flat-traps of to-day—disappeared. What happened was what will happen here when we abolish this degrading system of giving credit on the sanction of body warrants. What happened in Athens was that, although there were some fraudulent debtors, the public sentiment became strongly in favour of honesty, and it is agreed that the prophecies of Solon's failure were not made good, and " that a loan of money at Athens was quite as secure as it ever was at any time or place of the ancient world." Furthermore, it is acknowledged by the better authorities that what I expect and believe will happen in the mean streets of England when imprisonment for debt is abolished actually did happen in Athens, and, to use Grote's words, " the prohibition of all contracts on the security of the body was itself sufficient to produce a vast improvement in the character and conditions of the poorer population."

Of course, I am not putting forward " What the Archon Did " as an example to the Archons who Didn't of to-day. The theory of evolution teaches us that in two thousand years the Solon type must have improved, and that the Solon that we see in the latter-day arm-chair of State must be a far, far better thing than anything that obtained in Ancient Greece. Possibly, the world having no use at all for Solons, the type is extinct. Be that as it may, I am more than ever puzzled, since I have studied the records of " What the Archon Did," why we retain our system of imprisonment for debt. If the world had got so far in the question of imprisonment for debt five hundred years before Christ, why are we where we are now nineteen hundred years since the Master set before us the true doctrine of forgiveness of trespasses?

Chapter XV : *Concerning Orders in Council*

AN Order in Council is an order of the King acting by and with the advice of the Privy Council. When an Act of Parliament provides that an Order in Council is to have the effect of an Act of Parliament, it is to be read as one with the Act and the Courts must accept its authority. In practice neither King nor Privy Councillor plays any actual part in preparing the Order in Council. This is always drafted and settled by the department interested in it with the aid of their legal advisers, and it comes before a meeting of a few Councillors summoned for the purpose of giving it a purely formal blessing and issuing it to the world at large. To all intents and purposes Orders in Council to-day are Statutes made by Civil servants instead of Statutes enacted by Parliament.

During the war, and indeed during the years preceding the war, Parliaments, being largely in the pockets of Governments and naturally desiring to escape the labour of discussing details, got into the evil habit of delegating to the executive the power to make Orders in Council or rules and regulations for enforcing statutes. Instead of the Act of Parliament being as it was in former days a charter of rights and duties which our representatives had carefully considered and enacted, it was now merely a licence to bureaucracy to legislate and enact by Orders in Council upon some chosen subject which Parliament was too busy or indolent to discuss in detail.

Nowadays it is impossible for a citizen to know his statutory rights and duties by purchasing a King's Printer's copy of an Act of Parliament; he has to go to the Stationery Office and purchase a bundle of leaflets by means of which officials from time to time, according to their taste and fancy, cast new burdens upon the hump of the taxpayer. Indeed, he will be lucky if the young lady at the stationery counter can provide him with a complete collection of these official broadsheets for, the Civil servant takes an uncanny pleasure in cancelling and re-editing them, and it is difficult for anyone to keep up to date with the latest reissues. Some regulations which affect the lives of citizens are not made public—for instance, the Regulations made by the Registrar-General of Births and Deaths—but as a rule, if a citizen has leisure, patience, and industry, he can, with the courteous assistance of the handmaidens of the Stationery Office, make a fairly complete collection of any branch of Statute law.

So careless of liberty did we become during the perils of the war and so arrogant grew bureaucracy that some minor Courts refused to allow a citizen to argue that an official order was *ultra vires*, and some departments did not even go through the form of providing Orders in Council, but issued orders on their own by inserting them in newspapers as advertisements.

It is worth remembering, therefore, that although

they may be impaired by the vicious practices of departmental distention, there still remain to us in principle certain limits to the powers of officialism which the Courts of Law will define and enforce. It is still good law to assert that a Minister of the Crown has no greater powers than any other official and cannot fine or imprison us. Moreover, the old Common Law of England still stands, and " Proclamations by the King in Council have not the force of law." Henry VIII obtained powers to give his proclamations the force of law, but this was relinquished under Edward VI ; and in James I's reign it was settled that " the law of England is divided in three parts—common law, statute law and custom, but the King's Proclamation is none of them."

It will seem impertinent to a Victorian to write down this elementary proposition, but from a careful study of the infusoria of the Circumlocution Offices of Whitehall I am convinced that they are wholly unaware of any such legal principle, and that unless some public reference to it is made from time to time the bright and glorious generation who are going to inherit the glories of our kingdom will find that one of the jewels of their inheritance is missing, and when the Minister of the Crown in whose keeping it should be found is asked if he knows where it is, the answer will be in the negative.

Let me therefore remind my young readers that though appearances are somewhat against the truth of the proposition I am setting down, yet it is still law that " if the King or his Ministers issue a proclamation or order it can have no effect except in so far as it is authorised by Parliament." Even an Order in Council must have an Act of Parliament at the back of it, and it is still the duty of our Courts to "protect every citizen from an unjust usurpation of power on the part of the Executive."

That bureaucracy accepts this proposition or acts upon it is, of course, quite another matter. In 1919 the Food Controller thought it would be convenient to make orders regulating the distribution and sale of milk. He issued licences to take milk from one county to another on condition that the licensees would pay him twopence a gallon "to form a pool which might be drawn upon for other purposes later." In other words, the Food Controller levied money for the use of the Crown without grant of Parliament against the form and substance of the Bill of Rights in that case made and provided. The Minister of Food did not even take the trouble to obtain an Order in Council to regularise this tax, but merely issued notices and advertisements that he was after the twopence and meant to have it.

It may have been a very excellent scheme, as far as I know, and no doubt many small persons paid up, as the average man does pay up if he gets an official buff paper and has enough in his pocket to satisfy the demand. But when the Wilts United Dairies, Ltd., were asked for a little bill of £15,000, being their share of the twopences, they took counsel—very eminent counsel—to defend them in Court. Bureaucracy had, of course, the assistance of the Attorney-General and others, and for more than twelve months the matter was argued with great skill and learning from the Court of First Instance to the House of Lords, where it ended in a crushing defeat for bureaucracy. The twopence was held to be a tax that could not be levied except by direct statutory means, a proposition that to a Victorian seems too obvious to be disputed. It was indeed a glorious victory. Wilts wiped out Whitehall. And the moral of it is that if an Englishman has pluck and energy and puts money in his purse he can safely adventure in the Courts of his country against the brigandage of bureaucracy.

You might suppose that this was the end of the matter, but there you merely exhibit the simplicity of the common woolly taxpayer. No sooner does the highest Court of Law in the land declare and forbid the illegal acts of bureaucracy than the Barnacles get thinking. A little Bill is presented to the House, only a very little Bill, published by the Stationery Office and purchasable for the ridiculous sum of twopence, which if it is allowed to be pushed through the House of Commons without protest will prevent any further trouble of this nature.

The preamble admits in airy phrase that certain Ministers purported to act " in pursuance of powers " which they had not got and " granted licences " and " required payments " and " imposed charges " that they didn't ought to have done. Then the little Bill suggests that Parliament should enact that : " No proceedings whatsoever shall be instituted by any person in any Court of Law or before any other tribunal whatsoever for the repayment to him of any sums so levied." And this is not all, for even if an action for recovery of illegal charges has already begun this little Bill is to hold up its hand and stop it, and all proceedings now pending are to be " discharged and made void."

Of course, one would suppose that no free Parliament could ever pass such an Act ; but one never knows in these degenerate days what may happen ; indeed, the mere fact that such a Bill could be drafted and presented to the Commons of Great Britain shows the measure of the contempt of bureaucracy for its nominal master.

But I think that Parliament will uphold the authority of the Courts and refuse, even at some cost to the State, to whitewash the wrongdoers, for when I read these modern judgments of our greatest judges still upholding those eternal principles of justice and right action which we have inherited from our forefathers I am hopeful that, in spite of the degradation and deterioration which the world has necessarily suffered in the last few years, there is going to be a return to reason, sanity, and peace. In a different degree the same evils we have suffered from have been experienced by our forebears, and if we fight the good fight as they did we shall attain to something akin to their serenity of freedom.

Bolsheviks and Bureaucrats have one attribute in common. They have no use for Parliaments or Law Courts, and seek to dispose of them and commandeer their powers. A Victorian like myself, nurtured on Hallam and Macaulay, has probably imbibed with the historical milk and water of his early years a distaste for the stronger political vintages of both Bolsheviks and Bureaucrats. If the claims of the departmentalists of to-day to decree in detail the down-sitting and uprising of every citizen are well founded, then it seems very clear that the early historians have dealt very hardly with institutions like the Star Chamber and men like Strafford and Laud and unduly exalted the citizenship of John Hampden, who, after all, was a species of conscientious objector.

William Laud, Archbishop of Canterbury, was the apostle of Orders in Council. He saw in them a great weapon of power. The man was a perfect type of the high-souled Christian Government official. His education at Reading School and St. John's College, Oxford, gave him exactly that unworldly outlook on life that lends a charm of manner to the least competent Civil servant. Had he lived in our own time he would probably have entered the Civil Service direct instead of taking orders. Once installed in a Government office, he would have rapidly risen to the head of it by sheer determination to have his own official way and to uphold the rights and privileges of his department. Seated at the head of the Council board, he would have been surrounded by congenial colleagues ready to applaud his boast " that as long as he sat there they should know that an order of that Board should be of equal force with a law or an Act of Parliament." Pym quoted these very words of his to prove the charge against him that he was endeavouring by his use of Orders in Council " to introduce into this kingdom an arbitrary power of government without limitations or rules of law."

Reading Laud's trial at length, although I find no reason to alter my early views about the political iniquity of his ways, I can see that to moderns who have been literally nurtured by the Orders in Council of a Minister of Food it must be very difficult to understand the outcry made against that unhappy man. I am at least convinced that his real line of defence when brought to trial was not to deny Pym's charge, but to glory in it and to have shown by arguments and instances that the limitations and rules of law are fetters which must be struck off the limbs of bureaucracy if it is to move along its paths of destiny to the goal of absolute power.

Our thick-headed ancestors were not sufficiently advanced in economic and constitutional wisdom to appreciate the blessings of the Star Chamber and the thorough paternal control of great departmentalists like Laud and Strafford. The small-minded business men of the era chafed at the injury to the freedom of trade caused by monopolies and arbitrary proclamations. They believed that industry could be amply safeguarded by traders themselves. They could not appreciate the direction from above by which certain individual industrious manufacturers were subject to what they considered to be cruel persecutions, whilst others were assisted to facile wealth. Even men like Clarendon criticised unrestrained exercises of prerogative and alluded with respect to "those foundations of right by which men valued their security which were never to the apprehension and understanding of wise men in more danger of being destroyed." Clarendon would thoroughly have approved of Lord Buckmaster's judgment in *The Attorney-General v. Wilts United Dairies, Limited.*

But the unhappy Laud was born out of due time and lived in a perverse generation. Even those to whom he might fairly have looked for support were fearful of his Orders in Council. A careful consideration of the facts of his trial almost convince me that had he lived to-day his actions and ideals would have been better understood, he might have led the blameless life of the successful permanent official and died an honoured member of the Order of the British Empire.

For when you read the real facts about the Star Chamber in the light of the history of modern departmentalism it is almost difficult to accept the flamboyant phrases in which Hallam describes this hated tribunal: "where those who inflicted the punishment reaped the gain and sat like famished birds of prey with keen eyes and bended talons eager to supply for a moment by some wretch's ruin the craving emptiness of the Exchequer."

After all, an exchequer has to be filled before bureaucracy can empty it. Hallam's undignified language might be used by reckless hysterical people about our own latter-day tax-gatherers and land valuers and commissioners and those super-officials authorised to commandeer private property and themselves assess the compensation they think fit to offer for it. The point that Pym and Hampden and Hallam seem to have missed is better understood to-day. Unless a department has money to spend it cannot carry through its splendid schemes for human betterment. It is essential, therefore, to entrust the head of the department with power to issue Orders in Council so that he can carry out his beneficent schemes. The old idea that prevailed in Laud's day that it was more constitutional for Ministers to explain their schemes to Parliament and obtain the consent of the people to the details of carrying them out and finding money for them is fast becoming obsolete. The method of to-day is but a slight variation of the methods of Laud. A short Act of Parliament is certainly passed, but it gives power to the bureaucrat to issue Orders in Council, to make such decrees as he wishes against persons and property and enforce them by legal steps and by the indirect means of withholding licences and trade facilities which are more powerful sanctions in the industrial life of to-day than tipstaffs and handcuffs.

Whatever may be said against the harshness of its administration the Star Chamber, from the point of view of modern departmentalism, was a great institution. It had the courage of its convictions and the people it convicted were roundly dealt with. There was no mawkish sentimentality about the Star Chamber. It did not " wait and see " or mumble Pharisee phrases about the " consent of the Government." It did govern. It was independent of public opinion and was always ready to have its own way and " damn the consequences." Moreover, it paid its way and was solvent. In a word, it was the kind of first-rate Government department in which many cultured thinkers of to-day see the only hope of our social salvation.

And the greatness of the Star Chamber was based on Laud's scheme of making Orders in Council of equal force with laws made by Act of Parliament. It was a great missionary effort made by an earnest, righteous man who could not see that his ideals ran counter to the instincts of the humanity he doubtless intended to serve. When you read the story of his career it has a very modern ring about it. When he first took over his official duties he saw clearly the difficulties ahead of him. " I shall now have no exercise," he writes to Strafford, " but slide over in a barge to the Court and Star Chamber; and in truth, my Lord, I speak seriously, I have had a heaviness hang upon me since I was appointed to this place, and I give myself no account of it unless it proceed from an apprehension that there is more expected from me than the craziness of these times will give me leave to do."

It is the bitter cry of weary Whitehall. The same complaint that you may listen to any morning from your eminent friend Barnacle, C.B., as you journey together in your suburban train that has superseded the barge. The " want of exercise," the constant voyage from home to the office, the lament over the " craziness of these times," with which your Whitehall companion is probably as much out of touch as Laud was in his day, and in the background of both their minds splendid schemes of grafting vines on thorns and raising fig crops in thistle fields which will never come to fruition through the close-fisted stupidity of the village Hampdens who will not part if they can help it.

To a modern mind the trial of Laud and the charges in his indictment are difficult to appreciate. That there was a generation of Englishmen who considered it a crime for a Civil servant to issue and enforce Orders in Council is strange reading to-day. To mention only one class of evidence, there were some sixty witnesses who complained that their houses had been pulled down by order of the Star Chamber without compensation.

Now, at first sight this may sound harsh and illegal, but Laud's defence, from a modern departmental point of view, is without flaw. "I confess," he says to his accusers, with a note of pride in his voice, "I confess I did when I first came to be Bishop of London project the repair of that ancient and famous Cathedral of St. Paul ready to sink into its own ruins." He goes on to explain that in order to carry out this very necessary reform it was essential that houses built by sacrilegious hands on holy ground and others adjacent to these should be cleared away, therefore the Star Chamber ordered it to be done. Then, again, all this happened eleven years ago, and the time limited for complaint is six. This sound technical defence Laud did not press home because he considered he had a clear defence on the merits.

His real defence was that the direction to pull down the houses was confessed to be by the Committee, and therefore no personal responsibility rested upon him. In that dark age this illuminating line of thought had scarce dawned upon the world. The proposition that by forming a Committee an individual could do that which was wrong and it would be accounted right, or at least that no one would be responsible for the consequences of the wrong done, was not fully understood. The idea of limited moral liability so clear to Laud's mind was never properly grasped by his judges. Yet he put it in very simple, clear language before them: "The Lords of the Council," he said, "are in the ancient constitution of this kingdom one body; and whatsoever the major part of them concludes is reputed the act of the whole, not any one man's. And this I must often inculcate because I see such public acts like to be heaped upon my particular."

If you think of it, the whole practice of government by Orders in Council depends upon this basic principle, namely, that the responsibility of a department is departmental. If the responsibility for an injustice done were to be borne by the particular Civil servant who did the wrong, the effect would be very detrimental to departmental complacency. A public official responsible for the consequences of his own acts would be in no better legal position than any other citizen.

Thomas Wheeler, Michael Burton, and the fifty other greasy citizens whose houses had been demolished and businesses ruined by the Star Chamber in order that they might carry out Laud's pious and patriotic building scheme, had obviously no right to throw the personal responsibility for their little troubles upon Laud, who was, as he fully explained, merely the Chairman and mouthpiece of the Committee. It is true the scheme was his, and the credit and glory of the project of repairing St. Paul's he very properly took to himself ; but the Committee were obviously responsible for any wrong done in carrying out the scheme.

It is difficult to understand the antiquated ideas of our forefathers. In this happy age we know nothing of " arbitrary and tyrannical government against law." How such words could have been used, as they were, in the indictment against Laud, how any body of citizens could have considered him to be a perverter of the cause of justice and a traitor who deprived them of their lawful rights, it is impossible for an Englishman of to-day to conceive. For in the three hundred pages of evidence given against him you will find little to censure from the standpoint of latter-day bureaucracy.

Yet his actions created in the minds of many of his fellow-citizens bitter hatred and loathing. Harbottle Grimstone, M.P., amid much cheering, describes him in the Limehouse of the day as " the sty of all pestilential filth," and yet to modern eyes he appears a typical upright Civil servant, somewhat severe and autocratic, no doubt, but of impeccable honesty. The tragedy of his life was that he was born in an age when Englishmen were rabid defenders of their rights and liberties. To-day he would have been a dignified pro-consul presiding over a comfortable herd of faithful bureaucrats, and he might have issued as many Orders in Council as he pleased and no one would have dared to challenge their legality.

But these strange forebears of ours were seized with a wild terror that this man William Laud was out to destroy the foundations of the State. He and his system must perish or the liberty of Englishmen would be destroyed. And after a long and weary trial, having in the drama of it some of the outward trappings of justice, the end of the tragedy is realised : the scaffold is built, and on Friday, January 10th, 1645, the brave old man—he is in his seventy-second year—places his foot upon the rung of the last ladder.

He comes to his death like a true Briton, being fresh and cheerful, his " gallant spirit," so an old writer tells us, " being like the sun which shows greatest always at the setting." It is hard to believe that so brave and beautiful a spirit had inspired so much injustice, and it is impossible to-day to regard his death as anything but a judicial murder.

Yet the lesson of the tragedy has a grave meaning for modern Englishmen. The tendency of tired nations to hand over their liberties to officials accountable to no one but themselves, the craze in our own country for legislation by Orders in Council which during the war became a menace to our ancient liberties, the general decay of Parliamentary institutions, and the widespread evidences of unrest and revolution, are movements not wholly dissimilar from the social currents that swept over the country in the time of Laud.

One of the chief causes of industrial unrest in our own day has been the depressing effect upon the mind of man of departmental omnipotence. When the prayer of a poor ignorant person is unanswered or rejected without a hearing by a far-off Ministry, he becomes embittered and rebellious. To the man in the street the heads of the Circumlocution Office are as an unseen Providence whose decrees no one can resist.

As Job communed with himself about the Almighty, so thinks the weary citizen to-day of his own bureaucracy and so thought the aggrieved countrymen of William Laud.

> "For he is not a man as I am that I should answer him
> That we should come together in judgment;
> There is no daysman betwixt us
> That might lay his hand upon us both."

It is the absence of any appeal to any sort of daysman or arbitrator that makes departmentalism so hateful to English humanity. Every Order in Council that gives to unknown officials power to interfere with the works and doings of the common citizen is inflammable matter in the wrong place. Star Chamber powers, even in the hands of so pure and noble a man as William Laud, drove our countrymen to revolution. We shall be sinning against the light of history and running grave risks to the State if we continue to lower the currency of our Acts of Parliament by an undue alloy of Orders in Council.

Chapter XVI : *Concerning Coursing and the Law*

MOST people in these islands love some sport, and I confess to looking forward with youthful longing to a day at Altcar, eagerly watching the "greyhounds in the slips straining upon the start." Nor can I honestly say that I have any memories more pleasant than some of the famous courses I have seen on the level plains of south Lancashire.

But when my more cultured friends speak to me of the cruelty of the sport I can only hang my head and agree with them. For, indeed, in all sport it appears this element of cruelty exists. You cannot hunt your fox, or slay your pheasants and partridges, or hook your salmon without causing some pain and inconvenience to your victims. Truly, if sport is to succumb to kindliness, the one pleasure left to the sportsman will be the tickling of trout, a cunning enterprise for village children, but scarcely honourable for grown men. And how much cruelty posterity will deem permissible in the sport of the future it is hard to say, since I have read of those who believe that the feelings even of a vegetable may be hurt by our homely culinary practices. If this be so, the cook who boils the cauliflower without removing the sleeping caterpillar is in danger of double damnation.

Concerning Coursing and the Law

Thinking the matter over with as much honesty as a man can who has already arrived at a conclusion from the premises, I am inclined to think that the entertainment and pleasure I take in coursing is due entirely to the fact that I was brought up to the study and practice of the law. The analogies between coursing and the law are remarkable, and inasmuch as the meanest of human beings is of more account than the "coward hare," the inhumanity of the law is less excusable than the cruelty of my favourite sport.

I can see now that education—that curse of the young, unfitting them for high ideals—is at the bottom of my love of coursing. A lawyer is trained from his youth up to hunt the criminal and hound him to death, to sleuthfully pursue the flying debtor, to stalk the bankrupt to his lair. Too much of his education tends towards the ideal of the American Circuit Judge whose epitaph is written by Edgar Lee Masters:

> "I in life was the Circuit Judge, a maker of notches,
> Deciding cases on the points the lawyers scored,
> Not on the right of the matter."

The coursing Judge of Lydiate riding after the dogs—he, too, is a maker of mental notches, deciding with unerring technical skill the cases before him "on the points." But note the vital distinction between coursing and the law. In coursing, the "points" are the absolute essentials to a just and righteous decision. Would that it were so in law!

It was when I grasped this leading difference between coursing and the law that I saw how excellent a thing it was that a weary pedantic "maker of notches" in a Court inferior in jurisdiction, sanitation, remuneration, and every other good quality, should escape into the open air of the sea-blown fields of Altcar, to be reminded that we have one ancient judicial proceeding, still continuing in our midst, where the matter is decided promptly to the satisfaction of all by a judge chosen by the people from whom there is no appeal. It is this aspect of coursing that makes glad the heart of the lawyer.

Now that I have discovered this great truth and the real extent of the analogy between coursing and the law I shall cease to attend any coursing meeting as a pleasure, but continue my occasional visits as a duty, endeavouring to bring myself to a deeper knowledge and more intimate understanding of the mysteries of the sport, that I may bring these to bear on the problems of legal reform. In this way I begin to see that there is a great hope of such practical improvement in our legal system that the time will come when a lawsuit will be run off by a brace of counsel, and the judge will shout out the result in much the same time that is now occupied in a course on the Withens, and with the same satisfaction to everybody.

There are many traits in the character of King Solomon that are obviously not set down for the imitation of suburban man, but in connection with the subject in hand it is fit to remember that this estimable monarch was both an amateur judge and a keen sportsman. That decision of his in the porch of justice which settled the parentage of a baby is still quoted as a sporting judgment of wit and common sense. How long would such a parentage case have lasted to-day before our Courts of First Instance and Appeal?

That Solomon was a courser goes without saying. It has always been the sport of kings and princes. Hadrian had his Celtic hounds in his villa at Tivoli; at the Court of Charlemagne there were special officers, the Veltrarii, "in charge of the greyhounds"; the Anglo-Saxon dogs of Elfin Duke of Mercia are renowned in the history of coursing, and there have been many noble names among the nominators for the Waterloo Cup. There is, so far as I know, only one allusion to coursing in the writings of Solomon—namely, in Proverbs xxx., where he describes a greyhound as "comely in going." How certain is the Solomon touch—the words ring as true as Shakespeare's:

> ". . . like a brace of greyhounds
> Having the fearful flying hare in sight."

Or:

> "Thy wit is as quick as the greyhound's mouth: it catches."

Anyone who has watched the movement of a greyhound admiringly must admit that the words "comely in going" are descriptive poetical justice that could only have been uttered by a judge, a courser and a poet.

I know very well that the Splutterheims and Spitzbergs—the Boches of Biblical criticism—have decreed that our old English translation of the Hebrew word in Proverbs by "a greyhound" is all wrong, and that it should have been either a leopard, an eagle, a zebra, a cock, a wrestler, or a man in armour. They forget, or perhaps never knew, that Persia and Syria and the East were the earliest homes of coursing, and they had not the wit to see the subtle analogy between coursing and the law which makes Solomon's love of the sport the natural complement of his judicial wisdom.

Every author who writes of greyhounds breathes the joy and enthusiasm of the coursing field: from the eloquent and philosophic Flavius Arrianus—who in the days of Hadrian tells us that the sport of coursing and the breeding and management of the dogs was much as it is to-day—down to our own Shakespeare, with his yeoman love of a day off on Cotsall, when he put his money on the fallow greyhound, and all bets were off as the course "could not be judged." I ought, perhaps, to except Mr. Wordsworth from this category, but I doubt much whether he was a courser—a hound trail over Silver How was probably the extent of his sport; not but what that is an excellent day in the open. I have never been able to accept his account of the death of young Romilly, who tried to jump the Strid at Bolton Abbey and fell in and was drowned. You may remember that Wordsworth says he went into Barden Woods with

> ". . . a greyhound in a leash
> To let slip upon a buck or doe."

I do not know anything of this sport, but surely a brace of greyhounds would have been desirable? And this may have been in the mind of the greyhound itself—for these dogs are more sagacious than many wot of—if Mr. Wordsworth is right in his statement that

> ". . . the greyhound in the leash hung back
> And checked him in his leap."

Hanging back is utterly unlike the conduct of a greyhound, who is more likely to have jumped first and pulled the young man in. But I have a strong belief that Mr. Wordsworth is all wrong about the greyhound, and that if one could turn up the records of the inquest it would be found that young Romilly had taken a bulldog out with him, or something that could not jump. For the credit of the greyhound this case requires further consideration, and when I next go to Harrogate to take the waters I will run over to Bolton Priory and see what is really known about it on the spot.

But these desultory thoughts about the literature of coursing are leading me away from the main purpose of my writing, which I will set down here and now. The value of coursing to the community is that in its ancient practice and procedure it is a model of what the law might be if lawyers would humbly learn the lessons of the sport.

For regard the two greyhounds as litigants and the hare as a *chose in action* which both are eager to reduce into possession, or take it that the dogs are merely counsel and that the hare is the cause of action, or the issue between them, or the verdict or judgment they are pursuing: whichever way you look at it there, as in litigation in the Courts, are two contestants and a judge and a difficult proposition in the shape of a strong hare to fight about. Now, in the first place, in coursing the judge is a man chosen by experienced coursers to preside over the contest. He knows all the points of coursing—the go-by, the turn, the wrench, the trip, and the merit of the kill—and can assess their value unerringly and at once. Moreover, he is a man of such probity and wisdom that each opponent is ready to accept his decision without demur. It is clear that you could not be certain of obtaining a judge satisfactory to the coursing world by our present methods of judicial selection. Indeed, if Party services and business success in a profession were conditions precedent to the appointment of a judge at Altcar, coursing would soon see its last days.

Much might be learned by legal reformers from the way in which the judge in the saddle exercises his powers. For instance, there is a rule of coursing that " if a second hare be started during a course and one of the dogs follow her the course shall end there." I appeal to my brethren of the Bench and the Bar if this rule should not be added to the futile tonnage of Rules and Orders in the White Book. What an excellent thing it would be and how much money and time would be saved if in the course of a case when the counsel or litigant lost sight of the point and wandered after another—starting a new hare, as it were—the judge should declare him to be " unsighted " or non-suited, and in the words of the rule " the course should end there " and a new brace of litigants be called into the slips.

On the coursing field there is no such thing as " further consideration " ; there is no court of appeal, and the rule says that the " decision of the Judge once given shall not be reversed for any cause." If a nominator objects to any decision, the judge may be called on to explain it to the stewards of the meeting, who express an opinion as to whether it is satisfactory. This seems to me a procedure well worthy of consideration. If we had a committee of stewards to report on the justice of decisions without overruling the decisions, the necessity of pensioning undiscerning judges who failed to appreciate points would be as obvious in law as it is in coursing.

Much time, too, could be saved in the legal methods of giving judgment. At the end of the course the judge of a course, who has no pleadings before him and knows no owners' name, calls out the colour of the winning dog —" brindle " or " fawn "—or takes his hat off to signify that the course is undecided ; and then the red or white or blue flag goes up to indicate his decision to the world. How much simpler it would be if the judge on the Bench were to call out " snub nose " or " moon face " to announce that the plaintiff or the defendant had won, or gracefully raise his wig to signify a non-suit, whilst the Associate held up little coloured flags to show the bookmakers at the back of the court the result of the suit.

And the moral of the whole matter is that as long as the world is a world of sport and contest it should make its rules of sport and contest simple and straightforward, and choose a trusted arbitrator to decide the matter once for all and abide by his decision. And towards the perfection of brevity and certainty of decision the law might learn many lessons from the ancient and honourable traditions of coursing.

I bow to my friends who speak of coursing as a cruel sport—as, indeed, all sport implicating the life of animals must be—but I cannot find it in my mind to repent of the joy I take in it ; and I hold that Sir Thomas Elyot delivered a wise judgment when he wrote that " hunting the hare with grehoundes is a ryght good solace for men that be studiouse."

Chapter XVII : *Concerning William Henry Seward*

SEWARD, like Lincoln, is known to his countrymen and to the world as an able and upright statesman, but by the legal profession he should be remembered as a great advocate of abiding conscience and courage.

In the dramas of the law advocates are not always called upon to play leading parts. The hero or heroine of the litigation may be a plaintiff or defendant or even a prisoner, and the greatest advocate has often to be content with a first or second part in the play enacted in the Courts, being merely retained to "support," as they say in the theatre, some leading star who has got into the limelight of litigation. It is bad art and bad advocacy for one who is cast to "support" to be for ever jockeying for the limelight that belongs to the star or edging himself into the centre of the stage and stepping out of the picture to the detriment of the drama.

But there are occasions when the honour and dignity of the profession call upon the advocate to set aside his modest scruples and cast himself for a leading part. Such a moment came to William Henry Seward when he defended the negro Freeman in the little court-house of Auburn, the capital of Cayeiga County, in New York State, some seventy-five years ago.

Concerning William Henry Seward

Seward was born in Florida in 1801. He was the fourth of six children, two of whom were girls. His native place was but a little village in those days in the southern part of Orange County, not far from the New Jersey boundary. His father was a country doctor and did his best to give him a good education, but was unable to provide him with much money. He seems to have been an over-studious youth, desirous, no doubt, to make good account of his father's sacrifices. He is described as a thin, pale, undersized lad with red hair and sandy complexion, coming to Union College, Schenectady, in ill-fitting homespun clothing, well equipped in Latin, but this he declaimed in a rustic drawl which provoked the laughter of the class.

To improve his dress he had to run into debt, and this led to quarrels with his father, who would not—and probably could not with justice to the rest of his family—improve his allowance. At the age of eighteen aggrieved by his father's neglect, he determined to throw up his college career and made off to Georgia; here he obtained a post as head teacher in a new academy at a salary of eight hundred dollars a year. Proud of his appointment, he sent his father word of it, but the old doctor wrote to his employers that his son had absconded from college and upbraided him in violent language. The new principal of the academy was inclined to set his father's authority at naught and his employers were quite ready to retain him. But the persuasions of his mother and sisters overcame his rebel pride. He opened the new academy and carried it on until a successor could arrive and take his place, when he returned to Union College, continued his studies, and took his degree.

He was now apprenticed to an attorney and began his serious study of the law under John Anthon, the practice expert in New York City. Here, too, he finished his student days, was admitted to practice in 1822, and went into partnership with Ogden Hoffman, a celebrated criminal lawyer. This partnership only lasted for a few months, and he began to look round in the Western part of the state for new worlds to conquer.

What led him to Auburn is mere conjecture. One may like to think that he had already met and loved the charming Frances Miller, and it was her beauty that was the magnet. Or maybe it was the opportunity of business and that the offer of Elijah Miller, the fair one's father, was a lucky accident that led to romance. The recorded fact is that he now became Elijah's partner, with a guaranteed share of five hundred dollars a year.

Auburn was what was known as a county seat. Though but recently settled and still boasting few buildings other than log houses, it was a growing centre of business. Seward from the first was a successful defender of prisoners. It was a great time for an alert brain ready to seize on errors in indictments. One of Seward's early successes was in defending a thief for stealing a " piece of calico " and a " quilted " piece and proving that the calico was white jean and the quilting was really sewing. On such points did life and liberty turn in those early days.

He was soon able to pay his old college debts and he became a model citizen. He owned a church pew, joined the militia and went to the dancing assemblies, and at the age of twenty-three married Frances Miller, his partner's daughter, then a girl of nineteen. She was undoubtedly a young lady of exceptional education and unusual natural ability, and her father, who was a widower, seems to have thoroughly approved the marriage, but made the young people promise to remain with him at his home.

After his marriage the young lawyer became a very popular and respected figure in the Auburn world. He very early turned his attention to a political career, and both political parties were ready to welcome so promising an adherent. He did not neglect his profession, but openly admitted that he practised the law to supply bread and cheese for his family and munitions of war to carry on the political fight. His many triumphs as a Whig politician, culminating in his election as Governor of New York, are part of the history of his earlier political career which came to a sudden check in 1843.

He was still a leading member of the Bar in reputation, though not in practice when the waning fortunes of his party deprived him of office, and he returned once again to Auburn, hung out the old tin sign over his office, and announced that he was once more sitting at the receipt of legal custom.

It must be admitted that he took little or no pleasure in the joys of advocacy. He used to express wonder to his friends: "Why I alone of all the decayed dignitaries should be doomed to the treadmill!" He cast back jealous glances at his lost position. His soul craved for the popular applause and splendid triumphs of political leadership, and he would cry out in his bitterness: "I fear, I abhor, detest, despise, and loathe litigation!" But with all this he had many forensic triumphs and held high ideals of the duties and privileges of advocacy.

For a man of over forty to begin again at the bottom of the ladder in his native town after tasting the glory of public life and high official dignity, must have been a hard task, but Seward faced it bravely. He sat in his office ready to receive the farmers and listen to their complaints of broken fences and trespassing cattle. It was as if one of our own retired Lord Chancellors were to find himself back at the local Bar holding a trumpery case in some suburban County Court.

"I spend my days," he writes, "in my law office. I charge reasonable counsel fees, and they are cheerfully paid. My earnings thus far have been equal to the salary for an equal period while in office. My expenses are vastly diminished—I do not work hard, and especially devote myself as counsel; have no partner, and only one clerk. I may earn five thousand dollars this year in this way if business continues as it has begun. I have commenced paying interest on all my debts. The principal is too great to be affected by my sinking fund unless I shall earn more."

It was this heavy weight of debt, the legacy of political success, that burdened his life at this period, but he never allowed it to tempt him to make money by unworthy means. One of the noblest attributes of the man and the advocate was that at this very period, when financial reasons made it essential that he should quickly regain substantial and wealthy clients, he undertook with enthusiasm and vigour the defence of unpopular and obscure interests. Not for a moment did he allow his distaste for many aspects of his profession, nor his personal troubles and difficulties, to prevent him from exercising to the full, in the interests of the poor, his high talents as an advocate.

If one were to search among the rolls of advocates of all countries for the name of one who has most ennobled his profession by a dignified display of courage and independence, the choice might well fall on William Henry Seward.

The story of his defence of the negro Freeman was perhaps better known by students of my generation than it is to-day. Yet it deserves to be remembered, and the report of the trial is worthy of study by advocates of all time; not only for the fact that it is a stirring and exhilarating tale of heroic conduct, but because, as Mr. Gladstone rightly said, Seward's speech in Freeman's defence is the "finest forensic effort in the English language."

The story of the crime itself may be shortly told. On March 11, 1846, a horrible and unaccountable murder took place. Without provocation, with no motive of plunder or revenge, a negro, named Bill Freeman, entered the house of a farmer named Van Nest and killed him and his wife and child and his wife's mother. Wounded in the struggle, Freeman stole a horse to escape, stabbed it and killed it, stole another, and fled for thirty miles. He was easily traced and captured.

He made no secret of the crime and laughed unconcernedly in the faces of his captors. The sheriff's men had great difficulty to prevent the mob from lynching him. Seward was away from home, but his wife wrote to him about the tragedy and described the wild outburst of the mob in the streets as the constable dragged the wretched maniac past her door to the gaol.

Now hear Bill Freeman's story. A few years back he had been a bright, intelligent lad of sixteen. He was arrested for stealing a horse and tried and sentenced to five years' imprisonment on the evidence of a negro who was afterwards discovered to be himself the thief. Freeman continued to protest his innocence and worried his gaolers for his release. This was regarded as insubordination.

By way of discipline a warder hit him over the head with a board, splitting the board and rendering the wretched nigger stone deaf. From that time he became morose, sullen, and stolid. Repeated scolding and flogging did nothing to better his condition.

At the end of five years he was turned out in the world a maniac whose one idea was that the State had injured him and he would make the State pay, and kill everyone he could.

His first visit was to Mrs. Godfrey, the lady whose horse had been stolen. She gave the poor imbecile a few kind words and a lump of cake, and this generosity no doubt saved her life, for he seemed to forget his grievances and wandered away. The same evening he found his way to Van Nest's farm.

The medical evidence as to his insanity was conclusive and there was a history of insanity in his family. But the mob were determined he should die. The funeral of the victims at the Sand Beach church on the shore of the Owasco Lake was an occasion of deep and thrilling interest. A multitude of people flocked thither from Auburn and from the surrounding farms. Four coffins were ranged side by side in front of the pulpit, and over them the clergyman preached a sermon which closed with an eloquent appeal for vengeance.

The preacher was determined to lose nothing of this wonderful opportunity for enforcing his message. "If ever there was a just rebuke," he cries out to the mob in front of him, "if ever there was a just rebuke upon the falsely so-called spirit of the day, here it is! Let any man in his senses look at this horrible sight and then think of the spirit with which it was perpetrated, and unless he loves the murderer more than his murdered victims he will—he must—confess that the law of God which requires that 'he that sheddeth man's blood by man shall his blood be shed' is right, is just, is reasonable." Then, after a strong attack on the "anti-capital punishment spirit," he concludes his impassioned address by pandering to the basest fears of his congregation, crying out, "Why, none of us are safe under such a false sympathy as this! . . . I appeal to this vast assembly to maintain the laws of this country inviolate and cause the murderer to be punished."

This Christian message was printed and circulated broadcast among the men from whom the jury were to be chosen, and it was common talk that, whatever direction the judge might give, Freeman was to be found guilty and hanged.

This was the position when Seward returned home and learned the whole story of the murder. He was disgusted to hear that the popular anger, which had been aroused when it was announced that he was engaged for the defence of the wretched criminal, had been temporarily appeased by the assurance of his law partner that he would not accept a retainer.

But this denial Seward could not permit to pass uncorrected. As he wrote to his friend Weed: "There is a busy war around me to drive me from defending and securing a fair trial for the negro Freeman. People now rejoice that they did not lynch him; but they have all things prepared for an *auto-da-fé* with the solemnities of a mock trial. No priest (except one Universalist), no Levite, no lawyer, no man, no woman has visited him. He is deaf, deserted, ignorant, and his conduct is inexplicable on any principle of *sanity*. It is natural that he should turn to me to defend him. If he does, I shall do so. This will raise a storm of prejudice and passion which will try the fortune of my friends. But I shall do my duty. I care not whether I am to be ever forgiven for it or not."

As soon as he announced that he would appear for Freeman and defend him in Court he was assailed with abuse from the whole community. He was denounced as an enemy of the people. His friends reasoned with him. His enemies threatened him with ruin. The mob houted and yelled at him in the streets, and some of the basest of them pelted his little children with stones. But Seward the man of intellect, the courteous, silver-tongued advocate with a distaste for the coarse publicity of the Courts, was not to be turned from the path he had marked out for himself. He would uphold the tradition of honesty and courage that are the heritage of English advocacy and would appear for the prisoner, even though the heavens might listen to the prayers of the local clergy and fall upon him and crush him to dust.

One does not exaggerate our hero's danger. This, remember, was the America of Martin Chuzzlewit. The local magnates were men like that typical journalist Jefferson Brick, whose gospel was that " the libation of freedom must sometimes be quaffed in blood " ; like that splendid sample of native raw material Hannibal Chollop, " who invariably recommended, both in print and speech, the tarring and feathering of any unpopular person who differed from himself " ; and like Elijah Pogram, the Congressman, who eulogised these ruffians as " true-born children of a free hemisphere."

It was before a jury and audience such as these, chewing and spitting and jeering and cursing at him, that the grave, discreet advocate was to unfold the garment of wisdom and cast down the pearls of eloquence.

Seward's own view, no doubt a correct one, of the facts of the case was that " Freeman was a demented idiot made so by his treatment in prison, which had extinguished everything in his breast but a blind passion of revenge. He should be acquitted at once and with the public consent." He himself visited the man in gaol and endeavoured to converse with him. Several of his friends did the same, and he obtained the highest expert opinions about the man's insanity.

The evidence of insanity was so strong that the judge

first submitted to the jury the question whether or not the man was fit to plead, and the jury, against the weight of evidence and argument, promptly found that he was fit. On the 6th July, 1846, the actual trial begins.

The day arrives when the negro is carried to the little court-house. There is not a vacant inch of space outside the dock. The high priests of the mob attend the *auto-da-fé*, impatient for the sacrifice. The imbecile is asked to plead. The clerk shouts in his ear, " Guilty or not guilty ? " The wretch grins and mutters, " I don't know." Other questions are shouted at him, with similar result. He is incompetent to follow what is going on. The Court enters his plea as " Not guilty."

" Will anyone defend this man ? " inquires the Court. There is a pause of death-like silence. There are many members of the Bar present. David Wright, a senior and spokesman, rises and says that he will not take part in the trial, which is only a terrible farce. Like Pilate, he washes his hands of the affair. The mob murmur their content. There is a pause. No one else speaks. The Attorney-General arranges his papers as if to open the prosecution. The spectators look at each other in breathless silence. Will any lawyer dare to outrage and defy public opinion ?

Seward, pale with emotion, his features set with inflexible determination, rises and in a clear voice opens the drama : " May it please the Court, I shall remain counsel for the prisoner until his death."

A groan of indignation fills the Court. Order is with difficulty restored. The Attorney-General rises in his place. The play has begun. Day by day it continues, and, faithful to his trust, Seward, unsupported by human sympathy of any kind, stands by the dock and maintains his client's cause.

At length the hour comes for Seward to address the Court. Even those who had come to curse him remained to hang upon his lips as if drugged by the truth and beauty of his appeal. The opening passages of his speech are a manly exposition to his hearers of the duty of the advocate to defend the criminal, however degraded and horrible his crime. Before he opens to the jury the overwhelming evidence of Freeman's insanity he makes clear his own position as an advocate and a citizen.

"For William Freeman," he says, "as a murderer I have no commission to speak. If he had silver and gold accumulated with the frugality of Crœsus and should pour it all at my feet I would not stand an hour between him and the Avenger. But for the innocent it is my right, my duty, to speak. If this sea of blood was innocently shed, then it is my duty to stand beside him until his steps lose their hold upon the scaffold. . . .

"I should be guilty of murder if in my present relation I saw the executioner waiting for an insane man and failed to say or failed to do in his behalf all that the law allowed. . . .

"I am arraigned before you for undue manifestation of zeal and excitement. My answer to all such charges shall be brief. When this cause shall have been committed to you, I shall be happy indeed if it shall appear that my only error has been, that I have felt too much, thought too intensely, or acted too faithfully."

What heart could fail to be touched by the picture he

puts before his fellow-citizens of the loneliness of a human being whose duty calls him from the path of popularity?

"I have addressed my fellow-citizens," he says, looking at the hard, scowling faces around him, "in many various relations, when rewards of wealth and fame awaited me. I have been cheered on other occasions by manifestations of popular approbation and sympathy; and when there was no such encouragement I had at least the gratitude of him whose cause I defended.

"But I speak now in the hearing of a people who have prejudged the prisoner and condemned me for pleading on his behalf. He is a convict, a pauper, a negro without intellect, sense, or emotion. My child, with an affectionate smile, disarms my careworn face of its frown whenever I cross my threshold. The beggar in the street obliges me to give because he says 'God bless you' as I pass. My dog caresses me with fondness if I will but smile on him. My horse recognises me when I fill his manger; and even the toad that I spare in my walk seems to look up to me with gratitude. But what reward, what gratitude, what sympathy and affection can I expect here? There the prisoner sits. Look at him. Look at the assemblage around you. Listen to their ill-suppressed censure and their excited fears, and tell me where among my neighbours or my fellow-men, where even in his heart, I can expect to find the sentiment, the thought, not to say of reward or of acknowledgment, but even of recognition."

This description of loneliness in pursuit of duty loses its force to some extent by being printed and read. One wants the voice and manner of the advocate, the sight of the imbecile wretch behind him, the grim jury, and the hatred gleaming in the eyes of the expectant mob ; in two words, the actor and the scene. It is difficult to report fine advocacy ; the words of it may be set down, but the drama of it can only be interpreted in the mind of the reader himself.

One does not perhaps do one's duty to a great speech by disconnecting special passages of beauty from a complete and well-built piece of oratory and advocacy. The whole speech should be read through, for the comments and human appeal in it are doubly enforced by the reasoned argument contained in it. The peroration in the circumstances amidst which it was spoken seems to me still to ring nobly true, though it failed in its immediate purpose. Again he makes a last appeal to the better instincts of the jury.

" The circumstances," he rightly reminds them, " the circumstances under which this trial closes are peculiar. I have seen capital cases where the parents, brothers, sisters, and friends of the accused surrounded him, eagerly hanging upon the lips of his advocate and watching in the countenances of the Court and jury every smile and frown which might seem to indicate his fate. But there is no such scene here. The prisoner, though in the greenness of youth, is withered, decayed, senseless, and almost lifeless. He has no father here. The descendant of slaves, that father died a victim to the vices of a superior race. There is no mother here, for her child is stained and polluted with the blood of mothers and of a sleeping infant, and 'he looks and laughs so that she cannot bear to look upon him.' There is no brother or sister friend here; popular rage against the accused has driven them hence and scattered his kindred and people. On the other side I notice the aged and venerable parents of Van Nest and his surviving children, and all around are mourning and sympathising friends. I know not at whose instance they have come. I dare not say they ought not to be here. But I must say to you that we live in a Christian and not in a savage state, and that the affliction which has fallen upon these mourners and us was sent to teach them and us mercy and not retaliation.

" Although," he concludes, " we may send this maniac to the scaffold, it will not recall to life the manly form of Van Nest, nor reanimate the exhausted frame of that aged matron, nor restore to life, grace, and beauty the murdered mother, nor call back the infant boy from the arms of his Saviour. Such a verdict can do no good to the living and carry no joy to the dead.

" If your judgment shall be swayed at all by sympathies so wrong although so natural, you will find the saddest hour of your life to be that in which you will look down upon the grave of your victim and mourn with compunctious sorrow that you should have done so great injustice to the poor handful of earth that will lie mouldering before you.

" I have been long and tedious. I remember that it is the harvest moon and that every hour is precious while you are detained from your yellow fields. But if you shall have bestowed patient attention throughout this deeply interesting investigation and shall in the end have discharged your duties in the fear of God and in the love of truth, justly and independently, you will have laid up a store of blessed recollections for all your future days imperishable and inexhaustible."

The verdict was never really in doubt, and the jury, having found the poor wretch guilty of murder and rejected the plea of insanity, a day was fixed for sentence. Early on a July morning, when the rising sun had displaced the harvest moon, the eager crowd flocked to the Court-house to witness the last degrading scene of which but for Seward's action would have been a degrading legal drama.

The idiot, roused from his cell, was brought into the court-room and ordered to stand up. As he was nearly stone deaf, and the judge desired that as far as might be judicial things should be done decently and in order, he directed them to bring the prisoner close to the bench and, leaning over it, shouted to him:

"The jury say you are guilty. Do you hear me?"

"Yes," replied Freeman.

"The jury," repeated the judge, "say you are guilty. Do you understand?"

"No," said the negro.

"Do you know which the jury are?" inquired the Court.

"No," answered the prisoner.

"Well, they are those gentlemen down there," continued the judge, pointing to the jurors in their seats, "and they say you are guilty. Do you understand?"

"No."

"They say you killed Van Nest. Do you understand that? Did you kill Van Nest?"

"Yes."

"I am going to pass sentence upon you. Do you understand that?"

"No."

"I am going to sentence you to be hanged. Do you understand that?"

"No."

One cannot help thinking that by this strange dialogue the judge may have attempted, in no very direct or courageous method, to exhibit to the jury the folly of their handiwork. He did not go through the farce of addressing the prisoner further, but merely informed the mob and the jury that Freeman would be executed. There was only one person who received the announcement without any sense of emotion—probably he was too deaf to actually hear the words used—and that was the prisoner at the Bar.

Seward petitioned Governor Wright for a pardon, which was refused, but on appeal to the Supreme Court of the State a new trial was granted. The new trial was not proceeded with. The poor maniac died within a few months of the trial, and an examination of the brain disclosed proof of insanity.

The merit of Seward's conduct as a citizen and an advocate did not long remain unrecognised, and he soon regained and increased his practice at the Bar. In addressing the jury at the preliminary trial, when the jury had decided that Freeman was fit to plead, Seward had prophesied that "years hence, when the passion and excitement which now agitate this community shall have passed away, some wandering stranger, some lone exile some Indian, some negro, may erect over my remains an humble stone, and thereon this epitaph: 'He was faithful.' "

When in 1872 he passed away, full of years and honours, popular memory went back to that strange trial in the little Court-house in Auburn, and that the part played by their great fellow-citizen in the squalid and unhappy drama might never be forgotten, with one accord they placed upon his memorial the words he himself desired:

" He was Faithful."